PURE POULTRY

Cooking Arts Collection™

CREDITS

About the Author

Beatrice Ojakangas is a home economist, food consultant, teacher, recipe developer and food writer. She has written and published 23 cookbooks and numerous articles for national publications, and has appeared on PBS television with Julia Child on "In Julia's Kitchen with Master Bakers" as well as "Martha Stewart Living TV."

Currently, Beatrice is a columnist for the Minneapolis *Star-Tribune* and writes feature articles for the Duluth *News Tribune*. In her spare time, she teaches cooking classes. Besides a B.S. in Home Economics, she's done her graduate work in foods and nutrition, studied with Simone Beck in southern France at the LaVarenne, and at the Cordon Bleu in Paris.

PURE POULTRY

Copyright ©2000 Cooking Club of America

Mike Vail, Vice President, Product and Business Development
Tom Carpenter, Director of Book Development
Dan Kennedy, Book Production Manager
Jen Guinea, Book Development Coordinator
Tad Ware & Company, Inc.:   Book Design and Production
Photography
Food Styling
Recipe Testing

1 2 3 4 5 6 7 8 / 03 02 01 00
ISBN 1-58159-106-3

Cooking Club of America
12301 Whitewater Drive
Minnetonka, MN 55343

TABLE OF CONTENTS

NTRODUCTION

Today's chickens are descendants of wild fowl that roamed the dense jungles of primeval Asia. Chicken wasn't always as affordable as it is

today. In fact, for most of culinary history, chicken has been a luxury, making availability an appealing political promise. King Henry IV of France stated in his coronation speech that he hoped his people would have a "chicken in every pot every Sunday." Herbert Hoover made the same proclamation and political promise in the 1920s.

Back then, all you could find was the whole bird — especially those of us who raided our own chicken coops on Saturday for Sunday's dinner. But it's not just a whole bird scenario anymore. Today, most markets offer

mind-boggling choices. Not only is cut-up chicken readily available, but it comes marinated in dozens of flavors and ready-to-cook convenience.

Whole roasted chicken, flanked by gravy and mashed potatoes, coleslaw and biscuits, followed by apple pie for dessert, is almost a thing of the past, at best put into the category of "comfort food." Now, we're more likely to cook chicken pieces and flavor them in trendy new ways. But that works too. Compatible with a world of flavors, poultry products accept a rainbow of flavors… from the comfort foods of the past to the trendy, zesty, flavors that are popular today.

Poultry also offers a medium in which you can present the flavors of cuisines from around the world. From Mexico to the Caribbean, from South America to the Pacific Rim and into the rest of the East as well,

chicken and turkey are perfect for fusing world cuisine to that of our own by adapting flavor blends with the ingredients we have on hand.

Given the wide variety of chicken and turkey cuts available, you can even serve poultry dishes day after day without repetition. The possibilities are unlimited.

In addition, chicken and turkey are such lean meats that they can satisfy the requirements for low-fat and healthy meals. Small cuts cook quickly,

taking just minutes to prepare. And, best of all, both chicken and turkey are economical.

Pure Poultry will take you on a poultry-cooking journey. We'll start with the ins and outs and dos and don'ts of selecting, handling and storing chicken and turkey. Then we'll hit the kitchen, presenting dozens of recipes. Some are fancy, some are from points across the globe, some are just simple-but-great ideas you can prepare for dinner any weeknight. Altogether, it's *Pure Poultry*.

POULTRY ESSENTIALS

Great chicken and turkey meals begin long before you get out a pot or pan, or turn on the grill. This collection of advice, tips and techniques will help you choose the right bird or cuts for the task at hand, make sure the meat stays wholesome and full of flavor until you're ready to use it, and then prepare it properly for cooking.

Perfectly Simple Roasted Free-Range Chicken, page 113

CHICKEN ESSENTIALS

There are many choices when buying chicken today. You can select whole chicken, cut-up fresh chicken, boned chicken breasts or thighs, as well as marinated and fully-cooked chicken. If you're shopping for bargains, the more convenient the product, the more you pay per pound. For the best bargain and versatility in your menu, buy the whole bird and cut it up, marinate and cook it yourself. (See page 9 for instructions on cutting chicken; see page 142 for basic marinades.)

WHAT TO LOOK FOR

When selecting a whole chicken, look for a plump, blemish-free, smooth-skinned bird. When buying cut-up chicken, it should look fresh in the package. Boneless skinless chicken breasts and thighs should look pink and moist. Make sure the package is not torn or damaged, and check the "sell by" or "use by" labels. Chicken, whether whole or cut-up, spoils quickly, so be sure to keep it refrigerated and either freeze or use it before the expiration date.

HOW MUCH TO BUY

Allow about 1/2 pound bone-in, skin-on chicken per serving. For boneless chicken, plan about 1/4 pound per serving. Whole chickens are usually the best buy. And the bigger the bird, the more meat in proportion to bone.

BUYING THE WHOLE BIRD

- **Whole roasting chickens** are larger and older birds. They weigh between 4 and 5 pounds and can be up to 8 months old. A chicken that's labeled a "roaster" has a higher fat content, making it a good choice for rotisserie cooking, as well as for stuffing and roasting.

- **Broiler-fryer** is the most common type of chicken. The birds are young and weigh between 3 and 4 pounds and are usually about 2 to 2 1/2 months old. These chickens are named for their best uses — broiling or frying.

- **Stewing chickens** or hens range in age from 10 to 18 months and can weigh from 3 to 6 pounds. Their age makes them more flavorful but less tender. Cook stewing chickens with moist heat, such as stewing or braising.

- **A capon** is a rooster that is neutered when quite young, usually before 8 weeks, and is fed a high-fat diet. It is brought to market before it is 10 months old and ranges in size from 4 to 10 pounds. These chickens are full-breasted, tender and juicy, and are especially delicious roasted.

- **Rock Cornish game hens** usually weigh 1 to $1\frac{1}{2}$ pounds, but can weigh up to 2 to $2\frac{1}{2}$ pounds and are 4 to 6 weeks old. They're a hybrid of Cornish and White Rock chickens, and offer a relatively small amount of meat to bone. Each hen usually provides just enough meat for one serving. The larger ($2\frac{1}{2}$ pound) hens can be split, yielding two servings per hen. They are best broiled, roasted or grilled.

CUTTING UP CHICKEN

Cutting up your own chicken is more economical, and hand-cut pieces are more uniform with less torn skin. Follow these 8 steps to cut up a whole chicken:

1. Wash and dry chicken. Place on a sanitized cutting board with the breast side up.

2. Pull the leg away from the body of the chicken to find the joint that connects the thigh to the backbone. With a sharp knife or poultry shears, cut the leg and thigh away from the body by cutting through the joint. Repeat on other side.

3. To separate the leg and thigh, bend to find the joint, then cut through the joint to separate. Repeat this procedure for the other leg and thigh.

4. Pull the wing away from the body of the chicken to find the joint that connects the wing to the body. Cut through this joint with a knife or poultry shears. Repeat on other side.

5. Cut off the wing tip (save for soup or stock), and find the joint that connects the two wing parts. Cut through the joint with knife or shears.

6. Stand the bird upright on the neck end. Cut along each side of the backbone through the rib joints to separate the backbone.

7. Hold the breast with the skin side down. Cut through the cartilage at the V of the neck. Bend back both sides to pull and pop out the bone and cartilage. Pull out bone and cartilage. Cut the breast into halves.

8. To "fillet" a breast, slide your finger between the breast bones and the flesh of the chicken breast and pull bones away. Use poultry shears to snip the top of the breast bone away from the meat. To remove the "silver" tendon from the chicken breast, grab the tendon and pull it out of the breast meat, holding the meat back with thumb and forefinger.

BUYING CUT-UP CHICKEN

- **A quartered chicken** is cut into four pieces with each wing attached to a half of the breast, and each leg attached to a thigh. Quarters are perfect for grilling and barbecuing.

- **Pieces** consist of a whole chicken cut into 8 pieces: 2 legs, 2 thighs, 2 wings and the breast split into 2 pieces. The back and giblets are usually included in the package.

- **Breasts** may be whole (with or without ribs attached), split (with or without the ribs), boneless, or skinless and boneless.

- **A Tenderloin** consists of the part of the chicken breast that falls away from the larger boneless breast. It is usually small, slender, and very tender. Chicken tenderloins are most often available in frozen form or may be labeled "chicken for stir-frying."

OTHER CHICKEN CHOICES

What are the differences between the low-priced, abundantly available chicken we find in most meat cases, free-range chicken, organic chicken and kosher chicken?

- **Battery-Raised Chicken** — Most of the chicken we buy today in the United States is battery-raised. This means that chickens are kept in a confined space, fed and watered in their cages so that chickens can be ready for market as quickly and efficiently as possible. This chicken is economical, widely available and has tender flesh that cooks quickly, though it may lack flavor a little bit; at the least, it will need some of your culinary help.

- **Free-Range Chicken** — USDA standards state that to be labeled "free-range," chickens must have access to the outdoors. This is a broad definition that includes chickens that have had unlimited access to the outdoors as well as those that have only controlled access. Free-range chicken is usually available in all the ages, weights and sizes described already, but generally has more flavor because the chicken has had more freedom to go about being a chicken.

- **Organic Chicken** — True organic chickens are raised on pure grains and feeds, as opposed to processed food pellets. Organic chickens are usually free-range chickens as well.

- **Kosher Chicken** — Kosher chickens are raised and butchered according to rules governed by strict Jewish dietary law, and are approved and labeled as such. Kosher chicken is often free-range and organic as well.

TURKEY ESSENTIALS

Benjamin Franklin felt that the turkey should be our national bird. He was overruled, but not far from wrong when we consider the turkey's popularity for holiday meals.

Although the best selection of turkey is still available at holiday time, turkey isn't just for Thanksgiving anymore, nor is it just for a crowd of people. You can buy turkey whole in 4 to 6 pound sizes; you can stuff it or roast it or cut it up and grill it. Turkey parts offer versatility that grandma never had. Turkey is a lean, tasty bird that can be prepared dozens of ways — Benjamin Franklin would be proud!

Turkeys that are sold in supermarkets and meat markets are domesticated and are categorized by ready-to-cook weight. Plan on one pound of meat per person.

- Small — 4 to 10 pound turkey, 4 months old.
- Medium — 10 to 19 pound turkey, 5 to 7 months old.
- Large — 20 pounds and up turkey, 12 months old.

Hens usually have more breast meat and have smaller cavities, proportionately, than tom turkeys. All sizes can be either a hen or a tom turkey; read the label when purchasing if you have a preference.

WHAT TO LOOK FOR

Fresh turkey is much more succulent than turkey that has been frozen. Fresh turkey should be free of bruises and torn skin, and have a fresh, moist appearance. At home, rinse well inside and out, then pat dry before seasoning and preparing the meat for cooking.

When buying frozen turkey, check that it is well-wrapped and that no part of the turkey is exposed, subjecting it to freezer burn. Be sure to check the expiration date on the packaging.

In addition to whole turkey, look for both frozen and fresh turkey in the whole breast and half breast (bone-in or boneless), turkey drumsticks, thighs, hind quarters (thigh and drumstick), wings and drumettes (half wings), as well as turkey breast cutlets, slices and tenderloin.

Processed turkey products have greatly expanded the number of turkey items on the market. Turkey hams are interchangeable with regular boneless hams made of pork. Turkey sausages come in many different styles, from Italian to classic German flavors to Polish kielbasa. Cold cuts in various flavors are made with turkey. Thinly sliced smoked and flavored cooked turkey breast can be purchased at the deli counters of many markets.

THAWING

Place a frozen whole turkey (in its original wrapper) on a tray in the refrigerator. The tray will catch any drips. Be sure to allow the bird enough time to thaw completely in your refrigerator:

- 2 days for a 12-pound turkey.
- 3 to 4 days for a 24-pound turkey.
- To thaw turkey pieces, follow procedures on the packaging.

ABOUT STUFFING TURKEY

Do not stuff a turkey until *just before* roasting it. Stuffing provides the perfect moist and warm environment bacteria need to grow. Place stuffing into the turkey loosely so that the stuffing can expand as it absorbs juices. Ideally though, you should roast the turkey unstuffed (season the cavity with salt, pepper and herbs), and bake the stuffing in a separate pan.

COOKING TURKEY PIECES

As a general rule, slowly braise or simmer the dark meat (thighs, drumsticks and wings) until tender. The drumsticks contain many little bones that ideally should be removed before serving. You can roast white meat (breast) just like you would a whole turkey, and breast cutlets can be sautéed like boneless chicken breasts, broiled or cut up for stir-frying or kabobs.

WILD TURKEY

If you ever get a chance to cook and eat a wild turkey, do it. You don't have to be a hunter to appreciate the fuller, more robust flavor a wild bird offers.

The breast of a store-bought turkey is white when cooked; a wild turkey's breast meat is creamy-yellow colored, and has a more "intense" turkey taste. Take care to cook a wild turkey with a moist, gentle cooking method because the lean meat can dry out easily.

HANDLING RAW POULTRY PRODUCTS —
POULTRY COOKING SAFETY

Handle chicken like all food: safely! Did you know that improper handling and preparation of food (not just chicken) is responsible for 97 percent of all foodborne illness outbreaks? With chicken, usually it's because:

- The chicken was not handled properly during storage or cooking.
- The food preparation equipment was not properly cleaned.
- The chicken wasn't cooked long enough, or the holding temperature was too low.
- The raw chicken contained salmonella bacteria.

You can eliminate these health concerns with safe handling techniques and proper cooking methods:

- Rinse chicken and dry with paper towels before cooking.
- Wash your hands before and after handling raw chicken.
- Keep raw chicken wrapped and separate from other foods to eliminate the possibility of cross-contamination.
- Wash cutting boards and knives in hot soapy water after using, and scrub your hands thoroughly before and after handling raw poultry.
- Don't return cooked chicken, or any food, to a plate or container that held raw chicken.
- When finished preparing chicken, clean all working surfaces with a solution of one part bleach to four parts water. Leave solution on surfaces for 5 seconds before rinsing well with cold water.
- Never leave cooked or raw chicken at room temperature for more than one hour. Refrigerate it promptly because bacteria grows quickly at room temperature!
- Cook chicken thoroughly. It is not safe to cook chicken partially, then store it to be finished later.
- Cook chicken until juices run clear when the meat is pierced with a fork.
- If you stuff turkey or chicken, always do it *just* before cooking. *Do not* stuff poultry ahead of time.

NOTE: These same food safety rules apply to turkey as well as chicken.

COOKING POULTRY AND KEEPING IT LEAN

Here are some general tips for cooking poultry and keeping it lean and low in fat:

- Chicken and turkey are lean meats — that is, without the skin. The skin can protect the meat while it cooks, keeping it juicy. But don't eat the skin if you're concerned about fat; about 2/3 of the fat in chicken is in the skin.

- Grilling, broiling or roasting chicken allows the fat to drip away. When you're roasting a chicken, be sure to place the bird on a wire roasting rack.

- For an especially moist and juicy chicken, simmer the bird in a small amount of water or broth. The meat will be low in fat, and so will the dish if you discard most of the simmering liquid and replace it with a low-fat sauce.

- Wine, cranberry juice, lemon juice and low-fat yogurt are just some of the ingredients you can choose to create a delicious low-fat sauce.

- When browning chicken pieces, use a nonstick skillet and a vegetable oil spray.

- Season chicken by preparing a low-fat or fat-free marinade of herbs, spices and juices or wine.

FRESH VS. FROZEN POULTRY CUTS

Packaged frozen chicken and turkey pieces are a convenient way to keep a supply of your favorite poultry product on hand for quick meals. Both chicken and turkey can be purchased frozen, packaged in bulk.

Chicken and turkey parts available in frozen form are economical, and they are usually packed in bags, individually frozen, and often "ice-glazed" to preserve freshness. The label may say that the chicken has been treated with a salt solution; this is done to increase tenderness and to keep the frozen poultry products from deteriorating in storage.

When buying frozen poultry, be sure to check for freezer burn. Freezer burn appears as dry white edges on the pieces, and is the result of the product drying in the freezer. This problem may indicate that the product has been frozen for a long period of time, or frozen and thawed more than once. Freezer-burned poultry will have an off-flavor, though it may be safe to eat.

Poultry pieces available in a bulk frozen form include halved bone-in and skin-on chicken breasts, turkey breast, boneless skin-on chicken breasts, boneless skinless chicken breasts, chicken and turkey tenderloins, bone-in and skin-on thighs, boneless skinless chicken or turkey thighs, chicken drumsticks, turkey drumsticks and chicken wings… almost any variation you can think of.

STORING POULTRY

Proper storage is essential to retain poultry's quality and delicate flavor. Poultry can be kept safely in the refrigerator up to 2 days and in the freezer for 6 months. To refrigerate, wash in cold water, pat dry and wrap in plastic food wrap or foil. To freeze, wash in cold water, pat dry and wrap in freezer paper or foil, or place in heavy-duty plastic freezer bags. Try to wrap with a minimum amount of air trapped in the package. The freezer temperature should be 0°F or lower.

There's more to thawing frozen chicken than just pulling a package out of the freezer and leaving it on the countertop until dinnertime:

- In the refrigerator, place the package in a bowl to catch any drips. It takes 12 to 16 hours to thaw a whole 4- to 5-lb. bird. It takes 4 to 9 hours to thaw a cut-up chicken.

- For faster thawing, place the chicken into a large bowl or basin, cover the meat with cold water, and change the water frequently to keep it and the meat cold.

- Chicken can be thawed in the microwave. Place the chicken onto a microwave-safe plate, cover with plastic wrap and place into the microwave for the following times and settings. Rearrange the chicken frequently during the thawing time.

MICROWAVE THAWING CHART FOR CHICKEN

Cut of chicken	Defrost or Low (30%) power
Boneless breasts	9 to 13 minutes per pound
Chicken pieces	4 to 8 minutes per pound
Chicken quarters	5 to 9 minutes per pound
Whole chicken	5 to 9 minutes per pound

HOW TO BONE POULTRY FOR STUFFING

The classic galantine (pronounced "GAL-uhn-teen"), a poultry-wrapped paté, is made using a whole, boned-out bird. To bone out a bird may sound like a lot of work, but once you have mastered the technique, you can produce a very elegant dish that looks impressive on a buffet when serving a crowd.

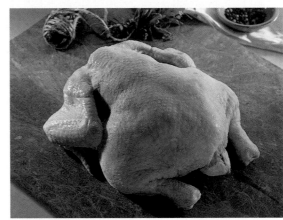

1. Place the bird, breast side down, on a sanitized work surface.

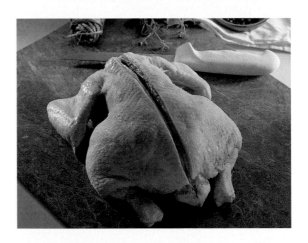

2. Using a sharp-pointed knife, make a cut down the center of the backbone through the skin, from the neck to the tail.

3. With the sharp edge of the knife always turned toward the bone of the bird, begin scraping the flesh off the bones, being careful not to cut into the skin, which will end up being the casing for the rolled, stuffed galantine.

4. Continue scraping the meat away, all the way to the breastbone, on both sides of the bird. Separate the wings and the thighs from the breast at the joint before lifting the entire breast and backbone from the meat.

5. At the wing, scrape away the wing meat from the bone all the way to the end of the drumette. With a pair of poultry shears, cut the tip and the next segment of the wing away and remove it. Repeat the procedure on the other side.

6. At the thigh, scrape the thigh meat away from the bone and remove the bone. Do the same with the leg; repeat on the other side of the bird.

HOW CAN YOU TELL WHEN POULTRY IS DONE?

USDA guidelines state that chicken or turkey should be cooked to 180°F. The best way to gauge doneness is by using a meat thermometer.

- **A regular meat thermometer** should be inserted into the thickest part of the inner thigh before you cook the bird. Do not let the thermometer touch bone or fat. The thermometer should remain there until it registers 180°F.

- **An instant-reading thermometer** is handy and easy to use and is a little easier to insert into a chicken because the probe is thinner.

Here's how to use an instant-read thermometer. Insert it into the thickest part of the inner thigh without touching the bone, and wait about 1 minute for the thermometer to register the temperature. Remove the thermometer from the chicken before returning the bird to the oven. Instant-read thermometers usually have plastic parts that will melt if subjected to oven heat.

To judge doneness without a thermometer, probe the thigh with a knife; when the juices run clear, the meat is cooked. Or cut between the thigh and the body of the chicken or turkey. The meat should appear cooked, not pink.

For cooking bone-in chicken or turkey pieces, you should be able to insert a fork into the meat with ease and the juices should run clear. However, the meat and juices nearest the bone might still be a little pink even though the chicken is cooked thoroughly. This happens especially if the poultry has been frozen for any length of time. The color is caused by hemoglobin, which is an iron-containing pigment located in red blood cells. The pinkish coloring is usually noticed in young chickens, which have less fat than mature chickens.

Thoroughly cooked boneless poultry pieces should no longer be pink inside. To check, simply cut into the piece with a knife.

EASY STEPS FOR CARVING POULTRY

Carving a whole chicken or turkey is quite easy. You'll end up with the following components: drumsticks, thighs (whole for a chicken or sliced for a turkey), wings, sliced breast meat. Here's how to get there, step-by-step:

1. Begin by removing the legs. Move a drumstick to locate the hip joint. With a sharp knife, cut through the tendons and joint to remove the leg. Repeat with the other leg.

2. Separate the thigh from the drumstick by cutting between them down to the joint. Cut through the joint and the tendons that surround it. Repeat with the other thigh.

3. You can leave a chicken thigh whole. When carving a turkey, slice the thigh meat.

4. Cut off the wings using the same method (above) as for removing the leg and thigh from the body of the bird.

5. Slice the breast meat in long, thin slices parallel to the rib cage. If carving a small chicken, you can remove the entire breast from each side, starting at the breastbone and cutting down along the ribs.

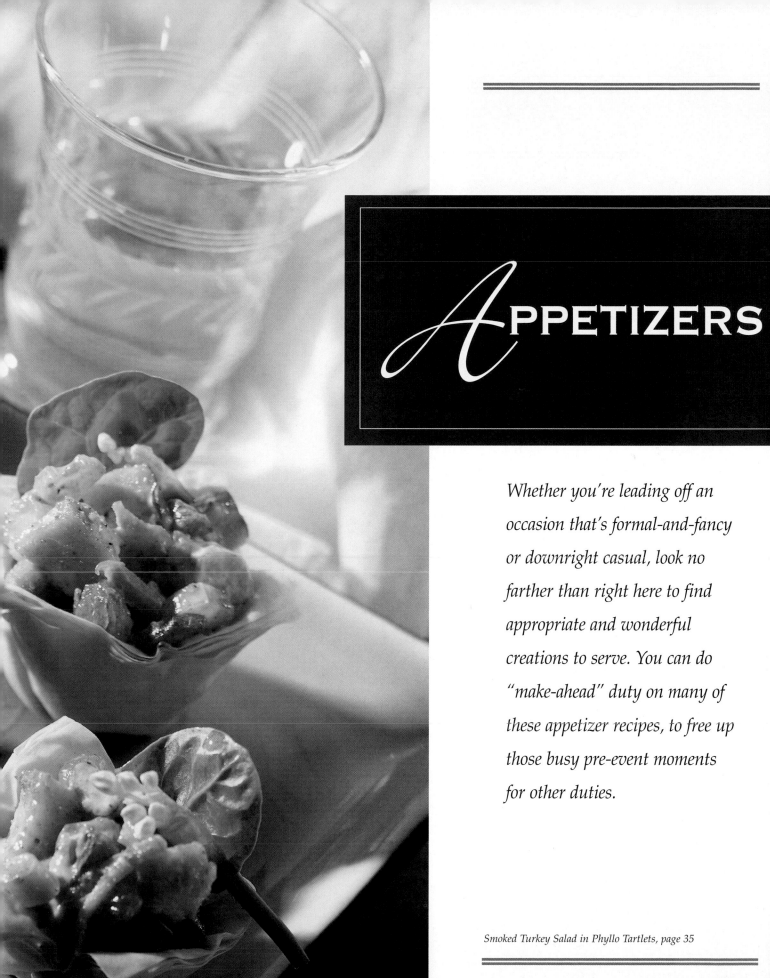

APPETIZERS

Whether you're leading off an occasion that's formal-and-fancy or downright casual, look no farther than right here to find appropriate and wonderful creations to serve. You can do "make-ahead" duty on many of these appetizer recipes, to free up those busy pre-event moments for other duties.

Smoked Turkey Salad in Phyllo Tartlets, page 35

ALMOND CHICKEN WINGS WITH PLUM ORANGE SAUCE

You can prepare these chicken wings before a party. Cook them just before serving, and reheat the sauce in the microwave to a warm serving temperature.

2½   lb. chicken wings, separated*
¾   cup all-purpose flour
1   egg, lightly beaten
1   tablespoon milk
¾   cup ground almonds
1   cup unseasoned dry bread crumbs
2   teaspoons salt
2   teaspoons grated orange peel
     Oil
     Plum Orange Sauce

❶ Rinse chicken and pat dry. In resealable plastic bag, toss chicken in flour, coat generously. In medium bowl, whisk together egg and milk; set aside.

❷ In another medium bowl, combine almonds, bread crumbs, salt and orange peel. Set aside.

❸ Dip chicken in egg mixture then almond mixture. Place chicken in shallow baking dish; refrigerate 30 minutes.

❹ In heavy skillet, heat oil to 375°F. Deep-fry chicken 10 to 15 minutes or until chicken is no longer pink in center. Drain on paper towels. Serve immediately with Plum Orange Sauce.

PLUM ORANGE SAUCE

$\frac{1}{2}$ cup orange marmalade
1 cup plum sauce or plum preserves
1 tablespoon cornstarch
1 tablespoon sugar
1 tablespoon rice wine vinegar or lemon juice
$\frac{1}{8}$ teaspoon cayenne

1. In microwave-safe bowl, stir together orange marmalade, plum sauce, cornstarch, sugar, vinegar and cayenne.

2. Microwave on High power 1 minute until sauce bubbles and thickens; cool.

3. Let stand 15 to 20 minutes. Serve warm as dip for Almond Chicken Wings. Extra dip can be covered and refrigerated up to 1 month.

TIP *See page 9 for directions.

12 chicken wings.
Preparation time: 1 hour. Ready to serve: 1 hour, 30 minutes.
Per serving: 270 calories, 11.5 g total fat (2.5 g saturated fat), 40 mg cholesterol, 510 mg sodium, 1.5 g fiber.

GARLIC-ROASTED CHICKEN BITES
WITH TEQUILA DIP

Fresh boneless chicken thighs taste the very best here, but the frozen variety will do. This looks like a lot of garlic, but it becomes quite mild during cooking. You'll smell it though!

2 teaspoons freshly ground pepper
1 teaspoon kosher (coarse) salt
1/2 teaspoon ground coriander
6 garlic cloves, minced
1 lb. boneless skinless chicken thighs, rinsed, dried, cut
    into 1 1/2-inch pieces
3 tablespoons minced fresh cilantro
   Tequila Dip

❶ Heat oven to 500°F.

❷ In medium bowl, combine pepper, salt, coriander and garlic; mix well. Toss chicken pieces in mixture until well coated. Coat 10x15-inch baking pan with nonstick cooking spray; arrange chicken in single layer in pan.

❸ Roast chicken 18 to 20 minutes or until no longer pink in center

❹ Sprinkle chicken with cilantro. Insert toothpick in each chicken bite; serve with Tequila Dip.

TEQUILA DIP

2 garlic cloves
1/3 cup ketchup
1 tablespoon packed brown sugar
1 tablespoon white or cider vinegar
1 tablespoon tequila or lime juice
1/2 cup raisins

❶ In food processor, combine garlic, ketchup, brown sugar, vinegar, lime juice and raisins; process until sauce is blended and raisins are coarsely chopped.

16 chicken bites.
Preparation time: 30 minutes. Ready to serve: 50 minutes.

Per serving: 70 calories, 2 g total fat (1 g saturated fat), 19 mg cholesterol, 175 mg sodium, 1 g fiber.

SATE SKEWERS WITH SPICY PEANUT SAUCE

Saté or Satay is an Indonesian favorite made of marinated, skewered meat, grilled and then served with a spicy peanut sauce.

- 4 boneless skinless chicken breast halves or 2 large turkey tenderloins, rinsed, cut into 1-inch cubes
- 1/4 cup Asian-style soy sauce
- 2 tablespoons vegetable oil
- 2 teaspoons minced fresh ginger
  Spicy Peanut Sauce
- 4 green onions, sliced (green and white parts)

❶ Thread chicken on short wooden skewers, 4 to 5 pieces per skewer. Place in single layer in large nonreactive baking pan. In small bowl, combine soy sauce, oil and ginger; mix well. Pour mixture over skewered chicken; turn to coat. Let stand 20 minutes, or cover and refrigerate up to 8 hours, turning skewers once.

❷ Heat grill. Place skewers on gas grill over medium-high heat or on charcoal grill 4 to 6 inches from medium-high coals. Cook 5 to 10 minutes or until chicken is no longer pink in center, turning once. Or heat oven to 450°F. Cook 5 to 10 minutes, turning once or until chicken is no longer pink in center.

❸ Transfer skewers to serving platter. Spoon Spicy Peanut Sauce over chicken; sprinkle with onions.

SPICY PEANUT SAUCE

- 3/4 cup chunky peanut butter
- 1 cup reduced-sodium chicken broth
- 2 tablespoons each packed brown sugar and lite soy sauce
- 1 tablespoon minced fresh ginger
- 2 teaspoons chile paste with garlic*

❶ In heavy saucepan, combine peanut butter, broth, sugar, soy sauce, ginger and chile paste; mix well.

❷ Simmer sauce, stirring frequently, about 2 minutes or until thickened. Serve hot or at room temperature.

TIP *Find chile paste in most Asian markets.

8 skewers.
Preparation time: 45 minutes. Ready to serve: 1 hour.

Per skewer: 250 calories, 15 g total fat (3 g saturated fat), 33 mg cholesterol, 430 mg sodium, 2 g fiber.

SPICY CHICKEN AND SHRIMP WONTONS WITH HOT CHILE DIPPING SAUCE

Cook these stuffed wontons in just a bit of oil, then steam. You can stuff wontons ahead of time; cover and refrigerate up to 6 hours before cooking and serving.

1/4 lb. ground chicken or turkey
6 medium uncooked shrimp, peeled, minced
2 garlic cloves, minced
2 teaspoons finely grated ginger
1 green onion, finely chopped
2 teaspoons chopped fresh cilantro
1 tablespoon sweet-hot Asian chile sauce*
1 teaspoon soy sauce
24 wonton wrappers
1 tablespoon vegetable oil
1/2 cup chicken broth
1/4 cup water
Hot Chile Dipping Sauce

❶ In medium bowl, combine chicken, shrimp, garlic, ginger, onion, cilantro, chile sauce and soy sauce; mix until well blended.

❷ Place 1 heaping teaspoon of mixture in center of 1 wonton wrapper. Dip finger in small bowl of water and lightly moisten edges of wrapper.

❸ Bring the sides of wrapper up around filling to make a point at the top; press sides together firmly and pleat. Repeat with remaining wrappers and filling. Recipe can be prepared to this point up to 6 hours ahead. Cover and refrigerate.

❹ Before serving, heat oil in heavy skillet over medium-high heat until hot. Place filled wontons in skillet; cook about 2 minutes or until browned on all sides.

❺ Add broth and water. Steam wontons 3 minutes. Serve hot with Hot Chile Dipping Sauce.

HOT CHILE DIPPING SAUCE

1/2 cup Asian-style soy sauce
2 tablespoons rice vinegar
2 tablespoons sweet-hot Asian chile sauce*
2 tablespoons shredded fresh ginger

1 In small saucepan, combine soy sauce, vinegar, chile sauce and ginger; bring to a boil. Remove from heat. Serve at room temperature.

TIP *Asian chile sauce is available in Asian markets and in the international section of large supermarkets.

24 wontons.
Preparation time: 35 minutes. Ready to serve: 40 minutes.
Per wonton: 45 calories, 1.5 g total fat (1 g saturated fat), 10 mg cholesterol, 250 mg sodium, 1 g fiber.

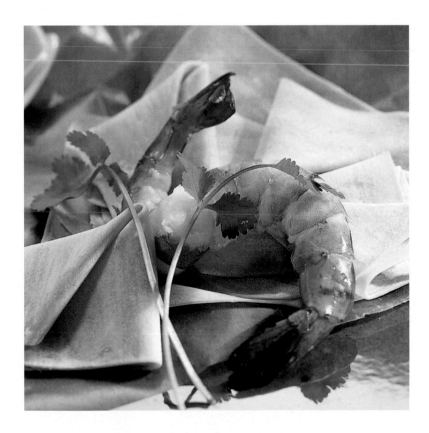

TURKEY TERRINE WITH PINE NUTS

Not just for appetizers, this terrine makes a great first course too! Slice and serve on a leaf of lettuce along with a tasty mustard. Or place thin slices on dark pumpernickel bread, spread with mustard and cut into small squares or triangles to serve as an appetizer or canapé.

2	tablespoons butter
1	onion, finely chopped
2	garlic cloves, minced
1/4	lb. fresh mushrooms, chopped
1/4	cup brandy
3	eggs
1	cup fresh whole-grain bread crumbs
1/2	teaspoon ground allspice
1/2	teaspoon dried thyme leaves
1/2	teaspoon salt
1 1/4	lb. lean ground turkey
1/2	lb. cooked turkey ham, cut into 1/2-inch pieces
2/3	cup pine nuts

❶ Heat oven to 325°F. Coat 6-cup loaf pan or heavy terrine with nonstick cooking spray. Cut strip of parchment paper the same length as the pan; place in pan, allowing excess to hang over edge.

❷ In heavy skillet, heat butter over medium-high heat until melted. Add onion and garlic; cook about 2 minutes or until onion is soft. Add mushrooms; continue cooking about 1 minute, stirring occasionally until liquid evaporates.

❸ Add brandy; simmer 1 minute.

❹ In large bowl, combine eggs, bread crumbs, allspice, thyme, salt and mushroom mixture; mix well. Add turkey, ham and 1/3 cup pine nuts; mix until well blended.

❺ Pack mixture into prepared pan. Top with remaining 1/3 cup pine nuts. Press overlapping parchment paper over top of meat mixture; cover tightly with aluminum foil or terrine lid.

⑥ Place pan in larger pan; add water to larger pan measuring about halfway up sides of smaller pan. Bake until an instant-reading thermometer inserted into the center of the loaf reaches 180°F.

⑦ Cool on wire rack. Cover meatloaf and chill thoroughly, at least 4 hours.

12 to 14 first course servings.
Preparation time: 2 hours, 30 minutes. Ready to serve: 4 hours.

Per serving: 210 calories, 13 g total fat (4 g saturated fat), 100 mg cholesterol, 370 mg sodium, 1.5 g fiber.

HONEY-SESAME CHICKEN TENDERLOINS

Add this to your party menu! The convenient chicken breast tenderloins frozen in bags at the supermarket are perfect to use in this recipe; if you prefer, cut chicken breast halves lengthwise into thirds.

1 lb. boneless skinless chicken breast tenderloins
1 teaspoon salt
2 tablespoons lite soy sauce
2 tablespoons honey
2 tablespoons dry sherry
1/2 teaspoon grated fresh ginger
1/2 teaspoon Asian five-spice powder
2 tablespoons vegetable oil
2 tablespoons sesame seeds
   Chopped fresh cilantro
   Plum Orange Sauce (page 25)

❶ Rinse chicken and pat dry. In shallow glass baking dish, combine salt, soy sauce, honey, sherry, ginger, five-spice powder and oil; mix well. Add chicken to mixture, turn to coat chicken evenly.

❷ Cover and refrigerate at least 2 hours or up to 8 hours, turning once or twice. Heat oven to 400°F. Sprinkle chicken with sesame seeds. Bake, uncovered, about 15 minutes or until chicken is no longer pink in center.

❸ Cut each piece in half (crosswise); place in serving dish. Sprinkle with cilantro. Serve with *Plum Orange Sauce*.

24 tenderloins.
Preparation time: 20 minutes.
Ready to serve: 2 hours, 25 minutes.

Per tenderloin: 30 calories, 1 g total fat (1 g saturated fat), 10.5 mg cholesterol, 50 mg sodium, 0 g fiber.

SMOKED TURKEY SALAD IN PHYLLO TARTLETS

This recipe, shown on page 22, makes an elegant appetizer or hors d'oeuvre to serve for a special party. You can bake the crispy phyllo "nests" a day ahead; just keep them in a cool and dry place, well-wrapped so they will not soften. The smoked turkey breast filling should be refrigerated. It's best to fill the cups just before serving.

5	sheets phyllo dough
2	tablespoons unsalted butter, melted
1/3	cup lite mayonnaise
2	tablespoons fresh lemon juice
1	tablespoon curry powder
2	cups finely diced, cooked, smoked turkey breast
1	carrot, finely shredded
1	rib celery, diced
1	tablespoon chopped golden raisins
1	tablespoon diced, roasted, red bell pepper
1	green onion, thinly sliced

❶ Heat oven to 350°F. Coat 24 miniature muffin cups with nonstick cooking spray.

❷ Brush 1 sheet phyllo dough with melted butter; top with another sheet phyllo dough and brush with butter again. Repeat until all 5 sheets are stacked. Cut stack into 30 squares, 5 rows by 6 rows.

❸ Press squares into prepared muffin cups, pressing pastry onto bottom and up sides of each cup. Bake about 8 minutes or until lightly browned. Remove from oven and cool in pan on wire rack; unmold. Bake remaining 6 nests. (You can prepare nests up to 24 hours before serving. Cover well, and store in a cool, dry place.)

❹ In medium bowl, combine mayonnaise, juice, curry, turkey, carrot, celery, raisins, pepper and onion; mix well. Cover and refrigerate up to 24 hours.

❺ To serve, fill each phyllo nest with 1 heaping tablespoon of mixture. Serve slightly chilled or at room temperature.

30 tartlets.
Preparation time: 30 minutes. Ready to serve: 24 hours.
Per appetizer: 35 calories, 2 g total fat (1 g saturated fat), 7 mg cholesterol, 130 mg sodium, 1 g fiber.

SOUPS

Just say "homemade chicken soup" and warm, cozy feelings encase you as you dream of a steaming bowl of that traditional, old-fashioned culinary remedy. The thought that somebody would make it for you probably has as much healing power as the soup itself! Make them with a little love, and these chicken and turkey recipes for the soup pot will create great feelings — and meals — too.

Turkey Stock, page 43

GINGER MISO CHICKEN SOUP WITH VEGETABLES

This is a flavorful veggie-filled chicken soup with an unthickened broth. Serve it as a first course when you're planning a meal for company, or for lunch any day.

1 (2½- to 3-lb.) frying chicken
2½ quarts water
1 tablespoon miso or chicken-flavored broth
½ cup chopped onion
½ teaspoon salt
½ teaspoon pepper
1 bay leaf
¼ teaspoon dried thyme
1 cup thinly sliced celery
1 cup coarsely shredded carrots
¼ cup green onion, diagonally sliced into 1-inch pieces
1 cup fresh snow peas or sugar snap peas

❶ In 8-quart stockpot, combine chicken, water, miso, onion, salt, pepper, bay leaf and thyme; simmer, covered, 45 minutes to 1 hour or until chicken is no longer pink in center.

❷ Remove chicken from broth; cool. Strain broth and remove fat from top of stock. When chicken is cool enough to handle, remove and discard skin and bones; shred meat into bite-sized pieces; set aside.

❸ Heat broth to boiling; add celery, carrots, green onion and peas. Simmer 10 minutes or until carrots are tender. Return chicken to broth; heat to serving temperature.

8 cups.
Preparation time: 30 minutes. Ready to serve: 2 hours.

Per cup: 115 calories, 3.5 g total fat (1 g saturated fat), 40 mg cholesterol, 285 mg sodium, 1.5 g fiber.

GRANDMA'S CHICKEN NOODLE SOUP

Comforting homemade soup may be just what the doctor ordered when you need it most. This is a soul-warming soup that you'll want to make over and over again.

2	tablespoons butter
1	small onion, finely chopped
1	carrot, diced
1	rib celery, finely chopped
1/4	cup all-purpose flour
2	quarts *Best Basic Chicken Broth* (page 42)
4	oz. dry egg noodles
1/4	cup half-and-half
1/2	teaspoon white pepper
2	cups shredded, cooked, chicken
	Freshly chopped parsley

❶ In 8-quart stockpot, heat butter over medium-high heat until melted; add onions. Cook 3 minutes or until tender. Stir in carrot and celery; cook an additional 5 minutes. Stir in flour; mix until well blended. Cook, stirring constantly an additional 1 minute.

❷ Add broth, stirring vigorously. Adjust heat to high and bring broth to boil. Add noodles and cook 10 minutes or until noodles are al dente.

❸ Stir in half-and-half, pepper and chicken; heat thoroughly. Garnish with parsley.

6 cups.
Preparation time: 18 minutes. Ready to serve: 30 minutes.

Per cup: 265 calories, 10 g total fat (4.5 g saturated fat), 67.5 mg cholesterol, 155 mg sodium, 2 g fiber.

CHICKEN CHILI SOUP WITH FRESH LIME

Spiced with chiles, a squeeze of fresh lime cuts the heat in this nontraditional chili.

2	tablespoons vegetable oil
3 to 5	jalapeño peppers, seeded, diced
1½	cups water
4	ripe tomatoes, halved, seeded, diced
1	small onion, diced
4	garlic cloves, chopped
4	cups *Best Basic Chicken Broth* (page 42)
3	boneless skinless chicken breasts, thinly sliced
3	tablespoons cornmeal
1	tablespoon chopped fresh cilantro
	Grated peel of 2 limes
	Juice of 1 lime
¼	teaspoon salt
¼	teaspoon freshly ground pepper
½	cup sour cream
1	lime, cut into wedges

❶ In heavy skillet, heat 1 tablespoon of oil over medium-high heat until hot; add peppers. Cook about 1 minute. Transfer peppers to small bowl; cover with 1 cup water and set aside 30 minutes.

❷ In food processor, process drained peppers, reserving liquid; process until smooth. Add tomatoes, onion and garlic; process until smooth.

❸ In 8-quart stockpot heat 1 teaspoon oil over medium-high heat until hot; add pepper mixture and cook 10 minutes, or until thick. Add broth and simmer, uncovered, about 30 minutes.

❹ In medium skillet, heat remaining 2 teaspoons oil over medium-high heat until hot. Add chicken and cook 4 to 5 minutes until chicken is no longer pink inside. Remove chicken from pan; set aside.

❺ Place cornmeal in small bowl. Add ½ cup water to cornmeal; stir until smooth. Whisk cornmeal mixture into simmering soup; add cilantro, lime peel and lime juice. Season with salt and pepper. Divide chicken among soup bowls; ladle soup over chicken. Garnish each bowl with dollop of sour cream and lime wedge; serve hot.

6 cups.
Preparation time: 30 minutes. Ready to serve: 1 hour.

Per cup: 290 calories, 13 g total fat (4.5 g saturated fat), 79 mg cholesterol, 505 mg sodium, 2 g fiber.

BEST BASIC CHICKEN BROTH

There's nothing better than homemade chicken broth. Best of all, you know what's in it!

3 to 4 lb. chicken bones or whole stewing hen, rinsed, cut up
    1 onion, quartered
    1 carrot, cut into chunks
    1 rib celery, cut into chunks
    2 sprigs parsley
    1 bay leaf
    1 sprig fresh thyme or $1/2$ teaspoon dried
    2 quarts cold water
  $1/4$ teaspoon salt
  $1/4$ teaspoon pepper

❶ In 8-quart stockpot, combine chicken, onion, carrot, celery, parsley, bay leaf, thyme, cold water, salt and pepper; bring to a boil over high heat. Reduce heat to low and simmer, partially covered, 2 to 3 hours or until chicken is no longer pink in center.

❷ Strain, discarding vegetables and bones. Pick large pieces of meat off chicken; reserve for making soup.

❸ Season broth to taste with salt and pepper. Cool; refrigerate until fat has congealed. Remove solid fat from top of stock; discard.

❹ Measure broth into heavy-duty resealable plastic bags and freeze flat.

4 cups.
Preparation time: 35 minutes. Ready to serve: 3 hours.

Per cup: 30 calories, 1 g total fat (0 g saturated fat), 0 mg cholesterol, 60 mg sodium, 1 g fiber.

TURKEY STOCK

Use the carcass of your Thanksgiving turkey to make a nice supply of stock for your freezer. Measure 2 cups of stock into pint-sized heavy-duty resealable plastic bags, freeze, and stack them like tiles on top of each other. Whenever a recipe calls for chicken or turkey stock, you've got a supply that you can trust!

1   carcass from large turkey, cut into 4-inch pieces
4   quarts water
3   carrots, cut into 2-inch pieces
3   ribs celery, cut into 2-inch pieces
2   onions, quartered
4   garlic cloves
1   small bunch fresh thyme (about 5 sprigs)
2   bay leaves, broken
1   bunch parsley

❶ In 12-quart stockpot, combine turkey, water, carrots, celery, onions, garlic, thyme, bay leaves and parsley; bring to a boil. Reduce heat to low; skim off fat. Simmer, partially covered 2 to 3 hours.

❷ Strain stock and discard solids.

❸ Refrigerate overnight; remove fat from top of stock. Refrigerate stock up to 3 days.

About 12 cups.
Preparation time: 35 minutes. Ready to serve: 12 hours.

Per cup: 25 calories, .7 g total fat (.2 g saturated fat), 0 mg cholesterol, 45 mg sodium, .2 g fiber.

CHICKEN MINESTRONE WITH TURKEY SAUSAGE AND BOW-TIE PASTA

Every cook has their own version of Minestrone. It may include sausage, meat or chicken, or it may be totally vegetarian. Ours includes chicken breasts and turkey sausage.

1/4	cup olive oil
1	onion, chopped
2	garlic cloves, minced
1/2	lb. boneless skinless chicken breast halves, rinsed and cut into 1/2-inch pieces
1/2	pound smoked turkey sausage, diced (1/2-inch thick)
2	carrots, diced (1/4-inch thick)
2	ribs celery, sliced
1	zucchini, cut in quarters lengthwise, sliced
3	cups green cabbage, shredded
6	cups *Best Basic Chicken Broth* (page 42) or 6 cups canned reduced-sodium chicken broth
1	(15-oz.) can cannellini or white navy beans, drained and rinsed
3/4	lb. red potatoes, scrubbed, diced (1/4-inch thick)
4	oil-packed sun-dried tomato halves, drained, minced
1	bay leaf
1/2	teaspoon dried thyme
2 1/2	teaspoons salt
1/4	teaspoon freshly ground pepper
1	(8 oz.) cup farfalle
	Freshly grated Parmesan cheese

❶ In a large stockpot, heat oil over medium heat until hot; add onion, garlic, chicken and sausage. Cook 7 to 10 minutes, stirring occasionally, until onion is golden and chicken is no longer pink in center.

❷ Add carrots, celery, zucchini, cabbage, broth, beans, potatoes, tomatoes, bay leaf, thyme, salt and pepper. Bring to a boil. Reduce heat and simmer, partially covered, until vegetables are tender, about 15 minutes.

❸ Remove bay leaf and add pasta. Simmer another 10 minutes until pasta is al dente. Sprinkle each serving with Parmesan cheese if desired.

8 to 10 cups.
Preparation time: 30 minutes. Ready to serve: 45 minutes.

Per cup: 330 calories, 13 g total fat (3.5 g saturated fat), 37 mg cholesterol, 1265 mg sodium, 6 g fiber.

CHEDDAR CHICKEN CHOWDER WITH POTATOES, CORN AND AVOCADO

Much like clam chowder, this soup is quick to make. It's wonderful on a blustery day. The suggested garnishes make this old-fashioned soup a new treat.

- 2 lb. boiling potatoes, peeled, diced
- 4 slices bacon, chopped
- 1/2 cup chopped onion
- 2 boneless skinless chicken breast halves, rinsed and diced (1-inch thick)
- 1 cup fresh whole kernel corn
- 3 tablespoons all-purpose flour
- 1 3/4 cups *Best Basic Chicken Broth* (page 42)
- 2 cups half-and-half

GARNISHES
- Chopped green onion
- Shredded sharp cheddar cheese
- Diced avocado

❶ Cover potatoes with water in medium saucepan. Cook over high heat until tender, about 20 minutes. Drain.

❷ In large stockpot, cook bacon, onion and chicken over medium-high heat, stirring occasionally, 10 minutes or until onion is tender, bacon is cooked and chicken is no longer pink in center.

❸ Pour off all but 2 tablespoons fat and stir in corn and flour; cook 2 minutes longer, stirring constantly. Add broth and half-and-half; bring to a boil.

❹ Stir in potatoes and heat to serving temperature.

❺ Garnish with chopped green onion, cheese and avocado.

6 cups.
Preparation time: 30 minutes. Ready to serve: 1 hour.

Per cup: 426 calories, 21.1 g total fat (10.4 g saturated fat), 66.9 mg cholesterol, 191 mg sodium, 4.3 g fiber.

SMOKED TURKEY, BROCCOLI AND BLACK BEAN SOUP

Don't let the long list of ingredients deter you. This colorful soup is really a snap to prepare!

1	bunch broccoli
2	tablespoons butter
1/2	cup chopped carrot
1/2	cup chopped celery
1/2	cup chopped onion
2	teaspoons dried thyme
2	teaspoons dried oregano
1	teaspoon dried basil
1/4	cup dry white wine
4	cups *Best Basic Chicken Broth* (page 42), or reduced-sodium canned broth
1	(16-oz.) can rinsed, drained, black beans
8	oz. smoked turkey breast, diced
1	tablespoon Worcestershire sauce
1/4 to 1/2	teaspoon cayenne
2	cups whipping cream
1/4	teaspoon salt
1/4	teaspoon pepper

❶ Peel and chop broccoli stems. In large stockpot, heat butter over medium-high heat until melted. Sauté broccoli stems, carrot, celery and onion in butter 5 minutes, stirring constantly.

❷ Stir in thyme, oregano and basil; reduce heat to medium and cook an additional 5 minutes, stirring constantly. Add wine and broth. Increase heat to medium-high; boil 15 minutes or until mixture is reduced by half.

❸ Add broccoli florets, beans, turkey, Worcestershire sauce and cayenne; simmer 5 minutes. Add cream; simmer an additional 5 minutes. Season with salt and pepper.

6 cups.
Preparation time: 30 minutes. Ready to serve: 30 minutes.

Per cup: 450 calories, 30 g total fat (18.5 g saturated fat), 114.5 mg cholesterol, 1140 mg sodium, 8 g fiber.

LEMON CHICKEN-LENTIL SOUP

For a soup with a warm, pinkish hue, try pink lentils in this recipe. Lemon lends a wonderful fresh taste and brings out the flavor of all the other ingredients.

        1 tablespoon butter
        1 onion, chopped
        3 carrots, chopped
        2 garlic cloves, minced
        1 cup dried lentils, rinsed*
        1 quart *Best Basic Chicken Broth* (page 42) or 2 (15-oz.) cans
               reduced-sodium chicken broth
        2 cups shredded, cooked, chicken
        2 tomatoes, diced
        2 tablespoons grated lemon peel
   1 to 2 tablespoons fresh lemon juice

❶ In 8-quart stockpot, heat butter over medium-high heat until melted; add onion, carrots and garlic. Cook, stirring frequently, 5 to 8 minutes or until vegetables just begin to brown.

❷ Add lentils and chicken broth. Bring to a boil; reduce heat to low. Cover and simmer 40 minutes or until lentils are tender.

❸ Add chicken, tomatoes, lemon peel and lemon juice; heat thoroughly.

TIP *Lentils are small, button-shaped beans that can be green, brown or pink. They have a distinctive but mild flavor, and a firm texture.

6 cups.
Preparation time: 40 minutes. Ready to serve: 1 hour.
Per cup: 255 calories, 6 g total fat (2.5 g saturated fat), 42.5 mg cholesterol, 100 mg sodium, 9.5 g fiber.

CHICKEN BOUILLABAISSE

Bouillabaisse is typically a humble fish stew made by fishermen on the beach, using the fish they weren't able to sell. This version uses chicken.

8   large chicken thighs
2   tablespoons olive oil
4   large garlic cloves, peeled, bruised
3   white onions, peeled, quartered
2   cups *Best Basic Chicken Broth* (page 42) or reduced-sodium
     canned broth
1   cup Madeira wine
3   sprigs parsley
2   bay leaves
1   thin strip orange peel
1/2   teaspoon saffron threads, or 1/4 teaspoon powdered saffron
     or 1/2 teaspoon turmeric
12   pitted green olives
6   large tomatoes, peeled, quartered or 2 (15-oz.) cans diced tomatoes
     Chopped, fresh parsley
12   slices French bread, toasted
     Rouille

❶ Rinse chicken and pat dry. Remove and discard skin and loose fat. In 8-quart stockpot, heat oil over medium-high heat until hot. Add chicken and garlic. Cook chicken about 6 minutes, turning frequently, until brown on both sides.

❷ Remove chicken and set aside. Add onions to pot; sauté 3 minutes, stirring frequently. Add broth, wine, parsley, bay leaves, orange peel and saffron; mix and heat to boiling. Return chicken to pot. Cover and simmer 45 minutes until chicken is no longer pink in center. Add olives and tomatoes.

❸ Pour soup into warm, deep, serving bowl and serve hot. Sprinkle with parsley. Place slice of bread in bottom of each individual bowl and ladle bouillabaisse over bread. Spoon rouille over each serving.

ROUILLE

$^1/_8$ teaspoon powdered saffron
2   tablespoons hot stock (from soup)
$^3/_4$ cup fresh French bread crumbs
1   large dried red chile, seeded
3   garlic cloves, peeled
$^1/_8$ teaspoon salt
$^3/_4$ cup olive oil

❶ Combine saffron, stock, bread crumbs, chile, garlic, salt and olive oil in food processor or blender. Process until thick, adding a little more hot broth from soup if necessary to make a smooth paste.

❷ Spoon over hot bouillabaisse.

6 cups.
Preparation time: 30 minutes. Ready to serve: 1 hour.

Per cup: 710 calories, 43.5 g total fat (7.5 g saturated fat), 83 mg cholesterol, 660 mg sodium, 5 g fiber.

SALADS

The lighter, whiter nature of chicken and turkey — along with the fact that they taste great cold — makes these meats natural accompaniments to (or centerpieces of) a wide variety of salads. The light and flavor-filled ideas here will quickly become natural parts of your salad repertoire.

Roasted Potato, Onion and Chicken Salad, page 60

GRILLED CHICKEN ANTIPASTO SALAD

Although there appear to be many steps to this salad, all the prep work can be done ahead of time. Just refrigerate the elements and put the salad together before serving.

- 3 red bell peppers
- 3 teaspoons olive oil
- 1/4 lb. Genoa salami, thinly sliced
- 2 tablespoons freshly grated Parmesan cheese
- 4 boneless skinless chicken breast halves
- 2 tablespoons olive oil
- 2 tablespoons fresh lemon juice
- 2 large garlic cloves, thinly sliced
- 1/4 teaspoon salt
- 1/4 teaspoon pepper
  - Kalamata Olive Dressing
- 1 lb. fresh baby spinach, washed, dried
- 2 small vine-ripened tomatoes, washed, quartered

❶ Heat oven to 500°F.

❷ Rub red bell peppers with 2 teaspoons olive oil. Line roasting pan with aluminum foil. Arrange bell peppers on pan; roast 10 minutes, turning frequently, until peppers have black spots and blisters. Remove peppers from oven and place in paper bag for 10 minutes. Peel off skin, remove stem and seeds; cut peppers into 1/4-inch strips.

❸ Reduce oven temperature to 425°F. Arrange salami slices in single layer on 9x13-inch baking sheet; sprinkle with Parmesan cheese. Bake 10 minutes or until browned. Drain on paper towels and cool; break into 1-inch pieces.

❹ Rinse chicken and pat dry. Heat heavy skillet over medium-high heat until hot. In small bowl, combine remaining 1 teaspoon olive oil, lemon juice and garlic; mix until well blended. Brush mixture over chicken; sprinkle with salt and pepper. Fry chicken on each side until chicken is no longer pink in center. Remove chicken from pan; cool and cut into 1/2-inch slices crosswise.

❺ Prepare Kalamata Olive Dressing. Arrange spinach on 4 individual serving plates or large platter. Top with tomatoes, roasted peppers and salami chips. Drizzle half of dressing over salad. Spoon chicken and remaining dressing over salad.

KALAMATA OLIVE DRESSING

    ¹/2 cup coarsely chopped brine-cured olives, such as nicoise
          or kalamata
     1 tablespoon chopped capers
    ¹/4 cup olive oil
     1 medium shallot, minced
     3 tablespoons red wine vinegar
     1 teaspoon Dijon mustard
     3 tablespoons finely chopped flat-leaf parsley

❶ In small bowl, whisk olives, capers, oil, shallot, vinegar, mustard and
parsley; mix until blended. Serve over spinach.

4 main dish servings or 8 first course servings.
Preparation time: 35 minutes. Ready to serve: 2 hours, 15 minutes.

Per serving: 600 calories, 44.5 g total fat (9 g saturated fat), 91 mg cholesterol, 1545 mg sodium, 5 g fiber.

CHICKEN COUSCOUS SALAD WITH BELL PEPPERS AND GARBANZO BEANS

Flavored with cumin, ginger, cinnamon and a touch of curry powder, this salad is a pretty shade of yellow. Prepare it up to 3 days ahead and refrigerate. Bring the salad to room temperature before serving.

2 cups *Best Basic Chicken Broth* (page 42) or 1 (15-oz.) can
    reduced-sodium chicken broth
3/4 teaspoon cinnamon
1/2 teaspoon each ground ginger, ground cumin and curry powder
3 tablespoons olive oil
1/2 lb. boneless skinless chicken breast
1 cup uncooked couscous*
1 carrot, diced (1/4-inch thick)
1 small red or yellow bell pepper, seeded, diced (1/4-inch thick)
1 small cucumber or zucchini, diced (1/4-inch thick)
1 small red onion, diced (1/4-inch thick)
1 small Golden Delicious apple, diced (1/4-inch thick)
1/3 cup raisins
1 cup canned garbanzo beans, rinsed, drained
1/2 teaspoon salt
1/4 teaspoon freshly ground pepper
1/4 cup freshly squeezed lemon juice

❶ Rinse chicken and pat dry. In saucepan, combine broth, cinnamon, ginger, cumin, curry powder, 1 tablespoon oil and chicken; heat to boiling. Simmer about 15 minutes or until chicken is no longer pink in center. Remove chicken; cool.

❷ Return mixture to a boil and slowly add couscous; stir and cook 1 minute. Cover and remove from heat. Let stand 15 minutes.

❸ Transfer couscous mixture into large bowl. Dice chicken into 1/2-inch pieces. Add chicken, carrot, bell pepper, cucumber, onion, apple, raisins and garbanzo beans to couscous; toss.

❹ Cover and refrigerate 3 hours. Season with salt, pepper and lemon juice before serving.

TIP *Made from durum wheat, couscous is precooked pasta used in Middle Eastern cooking. Substitute cooked rice for couscous, if you wish.

6 to 8 servings.
Preparation time: 40 minutes. Ready to serve: 3 hours, 30 minutes.
Per serving: 325 calories, 9.5 g total fat (1.5 g saturated fat), 20.5 mg cholesterol, 310 mg sodium, 5 g fiber.

ROASTED POTATO, ONION AND CHICKEN SALAD

While the potatoes roast in a hot oven, grill the chicken on a grill pan on the range. This is a really fast meal that's great for drop-in company — or last-minute planning!

2 lb. small red new potatoes, halved
4 small white onions, skinned, quartered
1/2 cup olive oil
1 tablespoon chopped fresh rosemary or 1 teaspoon dried
1 1/4 teaspoons salt
1 1/4 teaspoons freshly ground pepper
4 boneless skinless chicken breasts (1 1/2 lb.)
2 tablespoons red wine vinegar
1 teaspoon Dijon mustard
1 garlic clove, minced
2 tablespoons chopped fresh chives or green onion tops
1 basket (2 to 3 cups) cherry tomatoes, halved
3 cups mixed baby salad greens, washed, dried
1/4 cup pitted black nicoise or kalamata olives

❶ Heat oven to 450°F. In large bowl, toss potatoes and onions with 2 tablespoons oil, rosemary, 1/2 teaspoon salt and 1/2 teaspoon pepper.

❷ Cover bottom of large roasting pan with aluminum foil; coat with nonstick cooking spray. Arrange potatoes and onions in single layer. Roast, uncovered, 25 to 30 minutes or until potatoes are tender and onions are browned.

❸ Meanwhile, rinse chicken and pat dry. Coat chicken with 1 tablespoon oil; season with remaining 3/4 teaspoon salt and 3/4 teaspoon pepper. In heavy skillet, cook chicken over medium heat 5 minutes; turn and cook an additional 4 minutes or until chicken is no longer pink in center. Cool. Cut chicken diagonally into 1/2-inch slices.

④ In large bowl, whisk vinegar, mustard, garlic and remaining olive oil; mix well. Toss in potatoes, chives, tomatoes, greens and olives; mix well. Spoon mixture over chicken. Serve at room temperature.

4 servings.
Preparation time: 15 minutes. Ready to serve: 40 minutes.

Per serving: 290 calories, 13.5 g total fat (2.5 g saturated fat), 60 mg cholesterol, 145 mg sodium, 4.5 g fiber.

GRILLED CHICKEN AND SPINACH SALAD WITH RASPBERRIES

Grill the chicken either on the barbecue or a handy stovetop grill pan. When fresh raspberries are not in season, go for the individually frozen, unsweetened berries.

DRESSING
- 1 cup fresh unsweetened raspberries
- 1/2 cup orange juice
- 1/4 cup lemon juice
- 1 tablespoon honey
- 1/4 teaspoon salt
- 1/4 teaspoon freshly ground pepper
- 1/3 cup vegetable oil
- 1 tablespoon chopped fresh basil or 1 teaspoon dried

SALAD
- 2 (1/2-lb.) boneless skinless chicken breast halves
- 2 tablespoons extra virgin olive oil
- 3/4 teaspoon salt
- 1/4 teaspoon freshly ground pepper
- 8 cups washed, dried, baby spinach leaves
- 1 cup fresh unsweetened raspberries
- 1 cup seedless, halved, green grapes
- 1/2 cup chopped, toasted, walnuts or pecans

❶ In food processor, combine raspberries, orange juice, lemon juice, honey, salt, pepper and oil; process until berries are puréed. Strain mixture into container with lid. Add basil; cover and refrigerate 2 hours.

❷ Heat heavy skillet over medium-high heat until hot. Rinse chicken and pat dry. Brush chicken with oil; sprinkle with salt and pepper. Brush skillet lightly with oil. Place chicken, oil side down, on skillet. Brush top of chicken with remaining oil; sprinkle with salt and pepper.

❸ Cook chicken 5 minutes on one side; turn and cook another 5 to 10 minutes or until chicken is no longer pink in center, or an instant-reading thermometer reaches 180°F. Remove chicken from the skillet; cool. Slice crosswise into 1/2-inch pieces.

④ Divide spinach leaves among 4 salad plates. Top with raspberries, grapes and chicken. Sprinkle with nuts. Drizzle with dressing. Serve immediately.

4 servings.
Preparation time: 15 minutes. Ready to serve: 2 hours.

Per serving: 500 calories, 40 g total fat (5 g saturated fat), 33 mg cholesterol, 705 mg sodium, 6 g fiber.

SPICY ASIAN CHICKEN SALAD

This recipe has great flavor and a nice crunch. Visit your local farmers'
market for fresh bean sprouts, snow peas, onions and lettuce.

1   tablespoon Worcestershire sauce
3   tablespoons fresh lime juice
1/4 teaspoon cayenne
1   tablespoon sugar
1   tablespoon soy sauce
1   garlic clove, minced
1   lb. boneless skinless chicken breasts, rinsed and cut
       crosswise into 1/2-inch slices
2   tablespoons vegetable oil
3   cups rinsed, drained, fresh bean sprouts
1   cup snow peas, strings removed, trimmed
3   green onions, thinly sliced
1/2 small red onion, sliced 1/8-inch lengthwise
1/2 cup chopped fresh cilantro
    Lettuce leaves
    Lime wedges

❶ In medium bowl, whisk together Worcestershire sauce, lime juice,
cayenne, sugar, soy sauce, garlic and chicken; mix until evenly coated.
Let stand at room temperature 15 minutes.

❷ In heavy skillet, heat 1 tablespoon oil over medium-high heat until hot;
add chicken. Stir-fry chicken 2 minutes or until chicken is no longer pink
in center. Transfer chicken to large bowl.

❸ Add remaining 1 tablespoon oil to skillet and heat until hot, but not
smoking. Stir-fry bean sprouts, peas, green onions and red onions about
1 minute. Add vegetables and cilantro to chicken; toss well to combine.

❹ Line 4 salad plates with lettuce; divide among plates. Garnish with lime
wedges.

4 servings.
Preparation time: 10 minutes. Ready to serve: 20 minutes.
Per serving: 255 calories, 13.5 g total fat (2.5 g saturated fat), 22.5 mg cholesterol, 995 mg sodium, 2 g fiber.

CHICKEN, CORN AND BLACK BEAN SALAD

This colorful salad will be a favorite for outdoor summertime entertaining. Tote it to a picnic, or offer it on a buffet along with platters of sliced tropical fruits, cornbread and herbed butters.

4 1/2	cups cooked, diced, chicken
2 3/4	cups whole kernel corn cooked, drained, chilled
2	(15 1/2-oz.) cans rinsed, drained, black beans
1	cup diced red bell pepper
1	cup diced green bell pepper
1 1/2	cups thinly sliced green onion
2	tablespoons thinly sliced jalapeño pepper, seeded
2/3	cup pine nuts*

DRESSING

1/2	cup bottled hickory-flavored barbecue sauce
3/4	cup prepared Italian dressing (not creamy style)
2	tablespoons chili powder
1	tablespoon ground cumin
	Fresh lime juice
2 1/2	tablespoons chopped fresh cilantro
1 1/2	teaspoons hot pepper sauce

TO SERVE

Shredded Chinese cabbage or iceberg lettuce
Sour cream
Chopped black olives
Shredded cheddar cheese

❶ In large bowl toss chicken, corn, beans, red bell pepper, green bell pepper, onion, pepper and pine nuts; mix well.

❷ In medium bowl, combine barbecue sauce, Italian dressing, chili powder, cumin, lime juice, cilantro and hot pepper sauce; mix well.

❸ Pour dressing over mixture and toss to coat evenly. Refrigerate, covered, 3 hours. Serve on bed of shredded lettuce. If desired, garnish with dollops of sour cream, black olives and cheese.

TIP *Pine nuts are available in the bulk bins at supermarkets or at natural or whole foods cooperatives. They are also available in small bottles in the international foods section of many markets.

About 8 servings.
Preparation time: 10 minutes. Ready to serve: 3 hours.

Per serving: 480 calories, 21.5 g total fat (4 g saturated fat), 66.5 mg cholesterol, 610 mg sodium, 10.5 g fiber.

CURRIED TURKEY SALAD WITH MANGO AND TOASTED ALMONDS

This recipe is perfect for any time you have leftover turkey, and makes a lovely springtime luncheon. You might even roast a turkey just to have the cooked meat for this salad.

2½ to 3 lbs. cooked turkey breast, cut into bite-sized pieces
2 (8-oz.) cans water chestnuts, drained, slivered
1 lb. seedless green grapes, washed, halved
1 lb. seedless red grapes, washed, halved
½ cup raisins
2 cups sliced celery
2 green onions, sliced
2 cups toasted, slivered, almonds
3 cups lite mayonnaise
1 tablespoon curry powder
1 tablespoon soy sauce
2 tablespoons freshly squeezed lemon juice
1 lb. mixed baby lettuce greens, washed, dried
2 large mangoes, peeled, pitted, diced

❶ In large bowl, combine turkey, water chestnuts, grapes, raisins, celery, green onions and 1 cup almonds; mix well. In small bowl, combine mayonnaise, curry powder, soy sauce and lemon juice; fold into turkey mixture. Cover and refrigerate 2 to 4 hours.

❷ Arrange greens on large platter. Add turkey salad; sprinkle with remaining almonds and garnish with mango.

10 to 12 servings.
Preparation time: 15 minutes.
Ready to serve: 2 to 4 hours.

Per serving: 685 calories, 40.5 g total fat (6 g saturated fat), 107 mg cholesterol, 870 mg sodium, 7 g fiber.

RAISIN-SESAME CHICKEN SALAD

Bring home a deli-roasted chicken to get a great start making this salad. Nobody will know the difference.

2	cups shredded, cooked, chicken (about 2-inch pieces)
1/4	cup golden raisins
1/4	cup coarsely chopped toasted almonds
2	tablespoons soy sauce
1 1/2	tablespoons vegetable oil
1 1/2	tablespoons white wine vinegar
1	tablespoon sesame oil
4	cups shredded Chinese cabbage or iceberg lettuce
3/4	cup thinly sliced green onions
1/2	cup chopped fresh cilantro
2	oz. Chinese bean thread noodles
1/4	cup vegetable oil
	Toasted sesame seeds

❶ In large bowl, combine chicken, raisins and almonds.

❷ In another large bowl, whisk soy sauce, vegetable oil, vinegar and sesame oil; mix well. Pour half of mixture over chicken; toss chicken and set aside.

❸ Add lettuce, onions and cilantro to dressing; toss. Cut bean threads into 4 portions with scissors.

❹ In heavy skillet, heat oil over medium-high heat until hot. Add 1 portion bean threads. Fry until puffed; turn and fry other side until expanded. Drain on paper towels. Repeat with remaining threads.

❺ Assemble salad on four individual plates. Divide and layer chicken mixture and fried bean threads.

4 servings.
Preparation time: 15 minutes. Ready to serve: 25 minutes.

Per serving: 360 calories, 23.5 g total fat (4 g saturated fat), 56 mg cholesterol, 620 mg sodium, 2.5 g fiber.

SANDWICHES & SUCH

What's wrong with creating a sandwich for the sake of a sandwich? A great chicken or turkey sandwich can be so much more than just leftovers. The creative sandwich ideas here let the poultry — hot or cold — be the centerpiece and star! You'll also find some wraps, pizzas, and other casual foods.

Grilled Chicken, Cheese and Ancho Chile Sandwich, page 78

TURKEY HAM AND CHEESE BURGERS

A layer of ham and cheese in the center of each ground turkey patty makes this a great grilled sandwich in a bun.

1	lb. lean ground turkey
1	cup packed, finely chopped, fresh mushrooms
1/2	cup fresh bread crumbs
1	teaspoon onion salt
4	thin slices deli ham
4	thin slices mozzarella or Monterey Jack cheese
1/4	teaspoon salt
1/4	teaspoon pepper
4	large hamburger buns, split, buttered
2	tablespoons honey mustard
4	slices tomato
4	lettuce leaves

❶ In large bowl, combine turkey, mushrooms, bread crumbs and onion salt; mix until well blended. Divide mixture into 8 parts. Shape each part into patty about 4 inches in diameter.

❷ Top patties with one slice each of ham and cheese.

❸ Top with remaining turkey patties, sealing edges to enclose ham and cheese. Sprinkle with salt and pepper.

❹ Heat grill. Place patties on gas grill over medium-high heat; on charcoal grill 4 to 6 inches from medium-high coals; or on grill pan over medium-high heat. Cook 5 minutes on each side until turkey is no longer pink in center. Place turkey in hamburger bun and top with 1/2 tablespoon honey mustard, tomato and lettuce.

4 servings.
Preparation time: 10 minutes. Ready to serve: 15 minutes.

Per burger: 520 calories, 27.5 g total fat (11 g saturated fat), 114 mg cholesterol, 1165 mg sodium, 4 g fiber.

CHICKEN-PESTO MELTS

Use cooked leftover chicken, canned chicken, sliced deli chicken or turkey in these great melts. Or cook fresh chicken breasts and slice them for this quick-and-delicious sandwich.

- 2 boneless skinless chicken breast halves
- 1 teaspoon salt
- 4 teaspoons olive oil
- 4 slices French bread, cut diagonally and toasted
- 1 garlic clove, halved
- 4 tablespoons prepared pesto sauce
- 1 large tomato, cut into 4 thick slices
- 4 oz. sliced provolone, mozzarella or Monterey Jack cheese, sliced
- 4 sprigs Italian parsley

1. Rinse chicken and pat dry. Place chicken in heavy skillet; add salt and enough water to cover. Simmer over medium-high heat 15 to 18 minutes or until chicken is no longer pink in center. Cut chicken diagonally into thin slices.

2. Drizzle 1 teaspoon oil over each slice of toasted bread; rub each slice with cut side of garlic clove. Spread 1 tablespoon pesto over each slice. Top each slice with 1/4 of chicken, tomato slice, and 1/4 of cheese.

3. Heat broiler; broil slices about 4 inches from heat until cheese is bubbly. Garnish with parsley.

4 melted sandwiches.
Preparation time: 10 minutes. Ready to serve: 30 minutes.
Per sandwich: 365 calories, 24.5 g total fat (8 g saturated fat), 61 mg cholesterol, 620 mg sodium, 1 g fiber.

ERB-CRUSTED TURKEY CALZONE

Calzone is a stuffed pizza that originated in Naples, Italy, and resembles a large turnover. The fillings can vary from different kinds of meats to vegetables to cheese. If you have cooked turkey from a previous meal on hand, use about 2 cups of that meat instead of cooking the turkey called for here.

Herb Pizza Dough
4 tablespoons olive oil
1 small onion, thinly sliced
3/4 lb. boneless turkey breast, cut into 1-inch cubes
1 red bell pepper, seeded, cut into 1-inch pieces
1/2 cup dry white wine
1 tablespoon dried oregano
1/4 teaspoon salt
1/4 teaspoon freshly ground pepper
1/4 pound diced mozzarella cheese, diced

❶ Heat oven to 450°F. Prepare Herb Pizza Dough.

❷ In heavy skillet, heat 3 teaspoons oil over medium-high heat until hot. Add onion and cook 5 minutes stirring constantly, or until onion is brown and caramelized. Add turkey and bell pepper; cook an additional 5 minutes until turkey is no longer pink in center or internal temperature reaches 180°F. Add wine; sprinkle with oregano. Season with salt and pepper. Simmer about 30 minutes or until wine evaporates.

❸ Divide pizza dough into 4 equal pieces. On lightly floured board, shape each into circle about 6 inches in diameter.

❹ Place 1/4 of the turkey mixture on top of half of each circle, leaving 1/2-inch border. Top turkey with 1/4 of the mozzarella cheese. Brush edges of each circle with water; fold over to enclose the filling completely. Press edges together to seal. With fork, pierce top of each calzone to allow steam to escape.

❺ Place on lightly greased 9x13-inch baking sheet; bake 10 minutes. Reduce oven temperature to 400°F; bake 10 minutes or until crust is golden. Brush top with remaining oil and serve immediately.

HERB PIZZA DOUGH

1 pkg. active dry yeast
1 cup warm water, 105°F to 115°F
1 teaspoon oregano
1 teaspoon basil
1 teaspoon marjoram
1 teaspoon thyme
1 teaspoon rosemary
1 teaspoon sage
1 teaspoon fennel seeds
1 teaspoon salt
1 tablespoon olive oil
2¾ to 3 cups all-purpose flour

❶ To mix dough in bread machine, combine pizza dough ingredients in bread machine container. Program machine for dough cycle.

❷ To mix dough in food processor, measure dry ingredients in food processor bowl. With machine running, slowly add water through feed tube; process until dough cleans sides of bowl. Let dough rise in food processor 1 hour.

❸ To mix dough by hand, in a large bowl, dissolve yeast in warm water. Add remaining pizza dough ingredients except half of the flour. Beat mixture with spoon until smooth. Stir in remaining flour. Turn dough out onto lightly floured board; knead 5 minutes or until dough forms a smooth, round ball. Place dough in clean, lightly oiled bowl; turn dough over to grease top. Cover and let rise 1 hour or until doubled.

4 calzones.
Preparation time: 25 minutes. Ready to serve: 1 hour.
Per calzone: 680 calories, 25.5 g total fat (6.5 g saturated fat), 66 mg cholesterol, 785 mg sodium, 4 g fiber.

TURKEY CLUB WITH CRANBERRY AND BLT

This is a favorite day-after-Thanksgiving sandwich in many households. Some people like to add a layer of turkey dressing in place of the center bread slice in this triple-decker.

12   slices whole wheat bread, toasted
6   tablespoons butter, softened
3/4   cup whole cranberry sauce
8   lettuce leaves
1/2   lb. cooked turkey, thinly sliced
4   thin slices sweet red onion
8   slices cooked bacon

❶ Spread each slice of toast with 1/2 tablespoon butter and 1 tablespoon cranberry sauce. Layer toast, lettuce, turkey, toast, lettuce, onion, 2 slices bacon and toast for each sandwich. Cut sandwich into quarters to serve.

4 triple-decker sandwiches.
Preparation time: 5 minutes. Ready to serve: 5 minutes.

Per sandwich: 625 calories, 31 g total fat (15 g saturated fat), 104.5 mg cholesterol, 825 mg sodium, 7.5 g fiber.

GRILLED CHICKEN, CHEESE AND ANCHO CHILE SANDWICH

A sandwich filled with freshly grilled chicken breast and Southwestern condiments makes a tasty, satisfying and hearty meal. This sandwich is its best with freshly cooked chicken breast, but cooked, sliced turkey breast is also excellent.

2	boneless skinless chicken breast halves, rinsed, flattened*
1	tablespoon canola oil
1/4	teaspoon salt
1/4	teaspoon pepper
1/4	teaspoon chili powder
2	tablespoons butter, softened
4	slices wheat bread
4	(1-oz.) slices Monterey Jack cheese
2	teaspoons Ancho Purée
2	tablespoons sour cream
1/4	ripe avocado, thinly sliced
1	onion, sliced
2	tablespoons chopped fresh cilantro leaves

❶ Heat heavy skillet or grill pan over medium-high heat until hot. Brush both sides of chicken with oil; sprinkle with salt, pepper and chili powder.

❷ Cook chicken 4 to 5 minutes on each side or until chicken is no longer pink in center.

❸ Butter top of each bread slice. Place slice of cheese on unbuttered sides of 2 bread slices. Top with purée, sour cream, avocado, onion, cilantro and chicken. Top with remaining cheese slices and remaining bread slices, buttered side up.

❹ Grill sandwiches over medium heat until golden brown on each side.

ANCHO PUREE

        2 dried ancho chiles, seeded, stems removed
     1/2 cup hot water
     1/4 cup canola oil
        1 teaspoon fresh lime juice

❶ With scissors, cut chiles into pieces and drop into food processor. Add water and process about 3 minutes. With motor running, slowly add oil and lime juice. Refrigerate up to 2 weeks.

TIP *To flatten chicken breasts, place between sheets of plastic wrap and pound with flat side of meat mallet until about 1/3 inch thick.

2 servings.
Preparation time: 10 minutes. Ready to serve: 20 minutes.

Per serving: 760 calories, 51.5 g total fat (23.5 g saturated fat), 160 mg cholesterol, 1400 mg sodium, 6.5 g fiber.

BARBECUED CHICKEN WRAP

Flour tortillas are the perfect vehicle for wrap sandwiches, and there are several flavors to choose from. For a speedy sandwich, buy a barbecued chicken from the supermarket deli for the filling.

1½   cups shredded barbecued chicken
⅓   cup chopped romaine lettuce
¼   cup diced sweet red onion
1   cup chopped seeded cucumber
4   tomato- or herb-flavored flour tortillas (10 inches in diameter)
    Creamy Country Dressing

❶ In medium bowl, combine chicken, lettuce, onion and cucumber; mix well. Divide chicken mixture among tortillas, spread to within 2 inches of tortilla edge.

❷ Top each with 2 to 3 tablespoons dressing.

❸ Fold 1 end of tortilla 1 inch over filling; fold right and left sides over folded end, overlapping. Fold remaining end down. Cut in half to serve.

CREAMY COUNTRY DRESSING

1/2 teaspoon powdered mustard
1/2 cup heavy cream
  2 tablespoons fresh lemon juice
1/4 teaspoon salt
     Dash hot pepper sauce
1/3 cup lite mayonnaise

❶ In small bowl, whisk together mustard, cream, lemon juice, salt, hot pepper sauce and mayonnaise; blend until smooth.

4 servings.
Preparation time: 10 minutes. Ready to serve: 10 minutes.
Per serving: 400 calories, 23.5 g total fat (8.5 g saturated fat), 82 mg cholesterol, 720 mg sodium, 2 g fiber.

CARAMELIZED ONION, GORGONZOLA, ROSEMARY AND TURKEY PIZZA

Flour tortillas make a thin and crisp base for this California-style pizza.

1   tablespoon butter
2   large onions, thinly sliced
4   flour tortillas (8 to 10 inches in diameter)
1   cup (4 oz.) chopped, thinly sliced, cooked deli-style turkey breast
1   cup (4 oz.) crumbled Gorgonzola cheese
2   teaspoons chopped fresh rosemary or 1 teaspoon dried
1/4   teaspoon pepper

❶ In heavy skillet heat butter over medium-high heat until melted; add onions. Cook slowly, stirring frequently, until onions are browned and caramelized.

❷ Heat oven to 400°F. Arrange tortillas on large, ungreased cookie sheet. Bake 5 minutes.

❸ Spoon onions, turkey and Gorgonzola mixture over toasted tortillas; sprinkle with rosemary. Bake 8 to 10 minutes or until cheese is melted. Sprinkle with pepper. Cut into wedges to serve.

4 servings.
Preparation time: 5 minutes. Ready to serve: 15 minutes.
Per serving: 370 calories, 18.5 g total fat (8.5 g saturated fat), 50 mg cholesterol, 930 mg sodium, 3 g fiber.

CHICKEN QUESADILLAS WITH AVOCADO-TOMATO SALSA

When cut into eighths, these quesadillas make a wonderful appetizer!

　2　cups cooked, shredded, chicken
1/4　cup chopped fresh cilantro
　8　flour tortillas (8 to 10 inches in diameter)
　2　tablespoons vegetable oil
　1　cup shredded Monterey Jack cheese
　1　(4-oz.) can chopped green chiles, drained
　　Avocado-Tomato Salsa

❶ In small bowl, combine chicken and cilantro; mix well.

❷ Brush tortilla with oil. Top with 1/4 chicken mixture, 1/4 cup cheese and 2 tablespoons chiles. Spread mixture to within 1/2 inch of edge of tortilla. Top with another tortilla; brush top with oil.

❸ Brush heavy skillet with oil. Cook each quesadilla over medium-high heat 4 to 6 minutes, turning once after 2 minutes, until light golden brown.

❹ Cut each quesadilla on cutting board into quarters. Serve with Avocado-Tomato Salsa.

AVOCADO-TOMATO SALSA

  1 teaspoon ground cumin
  1 garlic clove, minced
1¹/₂ teaspoons fresh lime juice
 ¹/₂ teaspoon finely chopped jalapeño pepper
 ¹/₄ cup chopped green onions
 ¹/₄ teaspoon salt
 ¹/₄ teaspoon freshly ground pepper
  1 tablespoon chopped fresh cilantro
  1 cup finely chopped, drained, vine-ripened tomatoes
  1 small ripe avocado, peeled, pitted, finely chopped

1 In medium bowl, combine cumin, garlic, lime juice, pepper, onions, salt, pepper, cilantro, tomatoes and avocado; cover and let stand at room temperature 1 hour.

4 servings.
Preparation time: 15 minutes. Ready to serve: 1 hour, 10 minutes.
Per serving: 655 calories, 32.5 g total fat (9.5 g saturated fat), 83 mg cholesterol, 1450 mg sodium, 6 g fiber.

FAJITA CHICKEN IN PUMPKIN-SEED SAUCE

*When pumpkin seeds are puréed with green chiles and cilantro, they turn
into a delicate green sauce. These fajitas are great for a casual party menu.
Have guests spoon the chicken into warm flour tortillas and add toppings.*

1/2 cup roasted, salted pumpkin seeds*
1/4 cup blanched, slivered, almonds
1/4 teaspoon cumin seeds
1/2 small onion, cut up
 1 garlic clove
 1 (4-oz.) can chopped green chiles
1/2 cup packed fresh cilantro leaves
 2 cups chicken broth
 2 tablespoons olive oil
 4 large skinless boneless chicken breast halves, rinsed and
     cut crosswise into 1/2-inch strips
 1 tablespoon lemon juice
    Warm flour tortillas
    Shredded lettuce
    Chopped tomato
    Sour cream
    Sliced avocado
    Sliced jalapeño pepper

❶ In heavy skillet, cook pumpkin seeds, almonds and cumin seeds over
medium heat until toasted.

❷ Transfer mixture to food processor; add onion, garlic, chiles, cilantro and
1 cup broth, process until smooth. Set aside.

❸ Add oil to skillet and heat for 1 minute; add chicken, remaining broth,
juice and pumpkin sauce. Simmer, uncovered, 15 minutes or until
chicken is no longer pink in center.

④ Spoon chicken mixture into tortillas; garnish with lettuce, tomato, sour cream, avocado and jalapeño peppers.

TIP *Pumpkin seeds are available in whole foods markets as well as in bulk-bin sections of many large supermarkets.

4 to 6 servings.
Preparation time: 15 minutes. Ready to serve: 30 minutes.
Per serving: 575 calories, 30 g total fat (6.5 g saturated fat), 85 mg cholesterol, 1120 mg sodium, 500 g fiber.

MEALS IN MINUTES

The power of pieces comes into play. Instead of a whole bird, put that meat into smaller chunks and your cooking and preparation time goes way down. Most of these recipes will take you 30 minutes or less to create, less any marinating time, and some will be done in only 10 or 15 minutes! Best of all — these quick-and-savory ideas don't make you sacrifice any taste.

Mushroom-Sautéed Turkey Tenderloin, page 105

BASIC PAN-SAUTEED CHICKEN BREASTS

This is a basic method for a quick, delicious meal. Use this technique to make a world of different meals in less than half an hour. Flattened chicken breasts cook quickly. Once you've done it, you'll turn to this method over and over again. We offer six ideas to get you going, but you'll soon be creating your own! Buy boneless skinless chicken breasts or see this book's introduction for how to bone the breasts yourself (page 9).

4	boneless skinless chicken breast halves
1/4	teaspoon salt
1/4	teaspoon pepper
1	tablespoon vegetable oil
1 to 2	garlic cloves, minced
2	tablespoons broth

❶ Rinse chicken and pat dry; sprinkle chicken with salt and pepper. In large skillet, heat oil over medium-high heat until hot. Add chicken and garlic; cook, turning frequently, about 15 minutes or until chicken is no longer pink in center.

❷ Add broth to chicken; cook an additional 15 minutes.

4 servings.
Preparation time: 10 minutes. Ready to serve: 30 minutes.
Per serving: 175 calories, 7 g total fat (1.5 g saturated fat), 66.5 mg cholesterol, 385 mg sodium, 0 g fiber.

CHICKEN SAUTE WITH BASIL AND ASIAGO CHEESE

❶ Rinse chicken and pat dry; sprinkle chicken with salt and pepper. In large skillet, heat oil over medium-high heat until hot. Add chicken and garlic; cook, turning frequently.

❷ Add 2 tablespoons white wine, 2 teaspoons basil and 2 tablespoons freshly squeezed lemon juice to chicken. Cook about 15 minutes or until chicken is no longer pink in center.

❸ Transfer chicken to serving platter; sprinkle with fresh Asiago cheese.

4 servings.

Preparation time: 10 minutes. Ready to serve: 30 minutes.

Per serving: 200 calories, 8.5 g total fat (2.5 g saturated fat), 70 mg cholesterol, 450 mg sodium, 0 g fiber.

CHICKEN BREASTS WITH TARRAGON, MUSHROOMS AND GORGONZOLA

❶ Rinse chicken and pat dry; sprinkle chicken with salt and pepper. In large skillet, heat oil over medium-high heat until hot. Add chicken and garlic; cook, turning frequently.

❷ Add 1/2 lb. (8 oz.) cleaned and sliced baby mushrooms and 1/3 cup chicken broth to chicken. Cook over medium-high heat about 5 minutes, turning occasionally.

❸ In small bowl, combine 1/4 cup crumbled Gorgonzola, 1/4 cup heavy cream and 2 teaspoons dried tarragon; add to chicken. Cook chicken an additional 5 to 10 minutes or until chicken is no longer pink in center.

❹ Transfer chicken to serving platter; garnish with chopped fresh chives.

4 servings.

Preparation time: 10 minutes. Ready to serve: 30 minutes.

Per serving: 265 calories, 14 g total fat (6 g saturated fat), 89 mg cholesterol, 565 mg sodium, 1 g fiber.

CRANBERRY CHICKEN

❶ Rinse chicken and pat dry; sprinkle chicken with salt and pepper. In large skillet, heat oil over medium-high heat until hot. Add chicken and garlic; cook, turning frequently. *Continue with Step 2 on page 92.*

Continued from page 91

❷ Add 1/2 cup chopped green onion, 1 cup ketchup, 1/2 cup packed brown sugar, 1/2 teaspoon grated orange peel, 1 1/2 cups fresh cranberries and 1/2 cup cranberry juice to chicken; cover and reduce heat to low. Cook chicken an additional 15 minutes or until chicken is no longer pink in center.

❸ Transfer chicken to serving platter; spoon sauce over chicken. Garnish with chopped fresh cilantro.

4 servings.
Preparation time: 10 minutes. Ready to serve: 30 minutes.

Per serving: 365 calories, 7 g total fat (1.5 g saturated fat), 66.5 mg cholesterol, 1080 mg sodium, 2.5 g fiber.

CHICKEN BREASTS WITH WILD MUSHROOMS AND SAGE

❶ Rinse chicken and pat dry; sprinkle chicken with salt and pepper. In large skillet, heat oil over medium-high heat until hot. Add chicken and garlic; cook 7-10 minutes, turning frequently.

❷ Add 1/3 cup broth and 1/2 lb. sliced fresh wild mushrooms such as shiitake, chanterelles or portobello to chicken. Cook over medium-high heat, turning chicken, 2 to 5 minutes or until sauce is reduced to a glaze. Reduce heat to medium heat and cook an additional 5 minutes or until chicken is no longer pink in center. Stir in 1/4 cup heavy cream. Garnish with 2 tablespoons finely minced fresh sage or 2 teaspoons crumbled dried sage.

4 servings.
Preparation time: 10 minutes. Ready to serve: 30 minutes.

Per serving: 235 calories, 11.8 g total fat (4.5 g saturated fat), 82.8 mg cholesterol, 445 mg sodium, .8 g fiber.

CHICKEN IN CHAMPAGNE-CREAM SAUCE

❶ Rinse chicken and pat dry; sprinkle chicken with salt and pepper. In large skillet, heat oil over medium-high heat until hot. Add chicken and garlic; cook, turning frequently.

❷ Add 1 cup dry champagne, 1 teaspoon sugar, 1/8 teaspoon dried thyme leaves to chicken; cook 10 minutes. Stir in 1/2 cup heavy cream, salt and pepper to chicken; cook chicken an additional 5 to 7 minutes or until chicken is no longer pink in center.

❸ Transfer chicken to serving platter.

4 servings.
Preparation time: 10 minutes. Ready to serve: 30 minutes.

Per serving: 270 calories, 16 g total fat (7.5 g saturated fat), 99.5 mg cholesterol, 365 mg sodium, 0 g fiber.

BROWN-ALE SHIITAKE MUSHROOM CHICKEN

Brown ale gives the sauce a lovely, creamy tan color and an elusive but exciting bite. Quick to prepare; serve this with rice pilaf and stir-fried fresh vegetables.

2   tablespoons butter
2   tablespoons all-purpose flour
1/2 teaspoon salt
1/2 teaspoon pepper
4   boneless skinless chicken breast halves
31/2 oz. fresh shiitake mushrooms, sliced, stems removed
2   tablespoons finely chopped onion
1/2 cup brown ale
1   tablespoon Dijon mustard
1/2 cup whipping cream

❶ In heavy skillet, heat butter over medium-high heat until melted. In small bowl, combine flour, salt and pepper; mix well. Dip chicken into mixture and place in skillet. Add mushrooms and onions. Cook chicken about 20 minutes or until chicken is no longer pink in center.

❷ Add ale to skillet; cook an additional 5 minutes. Add mustard and whipping cream; simmer until sauce is pale tan and is consistency of heavy cream.

❸ Transfer chicken to serving platter; spoon sauce and mushrooms over chicken.

4 servings.
Preparation time: 10 minutes.
Ready to serve: 25 minutes.

Per serving: 304 calories, 18.5 g total fat (10.5 g saturated fat), 115 mg cholesterol, 305 mg sodium, 1 g fiber.

SPICY CASHEW CHICKEN STIR-FRY ON JASMINE RICE

To speed preparation, buy pre-cut vegetables. To add a bit more spice, sneak more cayenne into the sauce.

SAUCE
- 1 tablespoon cornstarch
- 1 cup chicken broth
- 2 tablespoons soy sauce
- 2 teaspoons minced garlic
- 1 teaspoon each curry powder*, cayenne

STIR-FRY
- 2 tablespoons canola oil
- 4 boneless skinless chicken breast halves, rinsed and cut into 2-inch x 1/2-inch strips
- 5 cups chopped fresh vegetables**
- 3 green onions, cut diagonally into 1 1/2-inch pieces
- 1/4 cup whole raw cashews
- 3 cups hot cooked jasmine rice

❶ In small bowl, combine cornstarch, broth, soy sauce, garlic, curry and cayenne; mix until well blended. Set aside.

❷ In heavy skillet, heat 1 tablespoon oil over high heat until hot. Add chicken and stir-fry about 5 minutes or until chicken is no longer pink in center. Transfer chicken to serving platter; cover.

❸ Add remaining 1 tablespoon oil to skillet; stir-fry vegetables about 2 minutes or until vegetables are crisp-tender and brightly colored. Add cornstarch mixture; cook about 30 seconds, stirring and tossing vegetables constantly until sauce is thickened and clear. Stir in chicken and cashews; serve with rice.

TIP *You can substitute 1/2 to 1 teaspoon crushed red pepper flakes and 1/2 teaspoon turmeric for curry powder.

TIP **Fresh vegetables may include broccoli florets, asparagus, snow peas, bell pepper strips, sliced celery or bok choy. Cut broccoli into florets; cut asparagus into 1-inch diagonal pieces; trim snow peas; cut bell peppers into strips and slice celery or bok choy diagonally.

6 servings.
Preparation time: 5 minutes. Ready to serve: 10 minutes.
Per serving: 315 calories, 10.5 g total fat (2 g saturated fat), 44 mg cholesterol, 875 mg sodium, 3 g fiber.

SWEET AND SOUR TURKEY TENDERLOIN

To add to the Asian theme, add a vegetable stir-fry to the menu. For dessert try coconut ice cream.

1 lb. turkey tenderloin
2/3 cup cornstarch
1/2 teaspoon salt
1 egg, beaten
5 tablespoons vegetable oil
1 medium onion, cut into 8 wedges
1 green bell pepper, cut into 1-inch pieces
1 medium tomato, chopped
1 (8-oz.) can pineapple chunks, drained
1/2 cup prepared sweet and sour sauce
3 cups rice, steamed

❶ Rinse turkey and pat dry; cut into 1½-inch cubes.

❷ In resealable plastic bag, combine cornstarch and salt; shake to mix.

❸ In large bowl, roll turkey in egg. Add turkey to cornstarch mixture in bag; shake until well coated. Set aside.

❹ In heavy skillet, heat 1 tablespoon of oil over medium-high heat until hot. Add onion and bell pepper; cook about 5 to 6 minutes, stirring occasionally. Remove from pan; set aside.

❺ Add remaining 1 tablespoon oil and turkey to skillet; brown and drain, if necessary. Add onion, bell pepper, tomato, pineapple and sweet and sour sauce. Cook until turkey is no longer pink in center.

❻ Serve over rice.

4 servings.
Preparation time: 10 minutes. Ready to serve: 15 minutes.

Per serving: 631 calories, 21.7 g total fat (3.9 g saturated fat), 93.8 mg cholesterol, 922 mg sodium, 2.3 g fiber.

TEN-MINUTE STIR-FRY CHICKEN AND VEGETABLES

The secret to great flavor here, as in all stir-fry dishes, is to have a really hot wok or skillet.

        4   boneless skinless chicken breast halves, rinsed and
              cut into 1½-inch cubes
        3   tablespoons cornstarch
        2   tablespoons peanut oil
        3   garlic cloves, minced
        5   tablespoons lite soy sauce
      1½   tablespoons seasoned rice wine vinegar
        1   sweet onion, thinly sliced
        2   (4- to 5-inch) zucchini, sliced diagonally lengthwise, halved
       ½   lb. sliced fresh mushrooms
       ½   teaspoon crushed Szechwan peppercorns
  ½ to 1   teaspoon crushed red pepper flakes
        1   large tomato, seeded, diced
            Steamed basmati or jasmine rice

❶ In large bowl, combine chicken and cornstarch; toss to coat.

❷ In heavy skillet, heat 1 tablespoon oil over medium-high heat until hot. Add chicken and garlic; stir-fry until chicken is no longer pink in center. Stir in soy sauce and vinegar. Transfer chicken to serving platter.

❸ Add remaining 1 tablespoon oil to skillet. Heat oil over high heat until hot; add onion, zucchini and mushrooms. Stir-fry until crisp-tender.

❹ Return chicken to skillet; season with peppercorns and red pepper flakes. Stir in tomato. Serve over rice.

4 servings.
Preparation time: 10 minutes.
Ready to serve: 10 minutes.

Per serving: 455 calories, 8 g total fat (2 g saturated fat), 66.5 mg cholesterol, 1430 mg sodium, 4 g fiber.

CHICKEN BREASTS STUFFED WITH GOAT CHEESE AND HERBS

Stuff and roll the chicken breasts up to a day ahead if you wish. You can even prepare the sauce in advance, but bake the chicken just before serving while you reheat the mushroom sauce.

4	boneless skinless chicken breast halves
1	(3½-oz.) pkg. fresh goat cheese, such as chevre or Montrachet
2	green onions, thinly sliced
3	fresh basil leaves, shredded or 1 teaspoon dried
1	tablespoon chopped fresh parsley
1	egg, beaten
½	cup dry unseasoned bread crumbs
2	tablespoons butter, melted
	Mushroom Sauce

MUSHROOM SAUCE

½	lb. sliced fresh mushrooms
1	cup *Best Basic Chicken Broth* (page 42) or reduced-sodium canned broth
1	cup heavy cream
1	tablespoon dry sherry
½	teaspoon dried thyme

❶ Rinse chicken and pat dry. Place each chicken breast between two sheets of plastic wrap. Pound with flat side of mallet to about ¼-inch thickness.

❷ In small bowl, combine cheese, green onions, basil and parsley; mix well. Spread mixture lengthwise over half of each chicken piece. Tuck short ends in and roll chicken up, starting at long side, to make long, tight cylinders.

❸ Dip chicken into beaten egg; roll chicken in bread crumbs. Place chicken in lightly greased 8-inch square baking dish. Drizzle chicken with melted butter. Cover and refrigerate up to 4 hours.

❹ Heat oven to 350°F. Bake 20 to 25 minutes or until chicken is no longer pink in center.

⑤ In medium saucepan, cook mushrooms and broth over medium heat about 8 minutes or until tender. Add cream; bring to boil until sauce is reduced and slightly thickened. Add sherry and thyme.

⑥ Serve chicken with Mushroom Sauce.

4 servings.
Preparation time: 30 minutes. Ready to serve: 4 hours, 30 minutes.

Per serving: 520 calories, 36.5 g total fat (21.5 g saturated fat), 198 mg cholesterol, 345 mg sodium, 1.5 g fiber.

HOT ROASTED CHICKEN AND POTATOES

If your family loves take-out fried chicken, they will love this even more! Cook potatoes at the same time in the hot oven, and you've got a meal that's delicious, as well as very healthy and low in fat.

1¹/₂	lb. boneless skinless chicken thighs
5	tablespoons olive oil
¹/₃	cup brown rice flour
1¹/₂	teaspoons salt
¹/₄	teaspoon freshly ground pepper
¹/₄	teaspoon dried rosemary
2	lb. potatoes, cut into spears
2	teaspoons kosher (coarse) salt

❶ Heat oven to 550°F. Rinse chicken and pat dry. Brush with 2 tablespoons oil.

❷ In medium bowl, combine flour, salt, pepper and rosemary; mix well. Toss chicken in mixture until coated.

❸ In another medium bowl, toss potatoes with 3 tablespoons oil; sprinkle with salt.

❹ Cover large, shallow, heavy roasting pan with aluminum foil. Arrange chicken pieces and potato wedges on foil.

❺ Roast chicken and potatoes 20 minutes or until chicken is no longer pink in center.

4 to 6 servings.
Preparation time: 10 minutes. Ready to serve: 20 minutes.

Per serving: 535 calories, 24.5 g total fat (4.5 g saturated fat), 75 mg cholesterol, 1295 mg sodium, 4.5 g fiber.

PEPPERCORN CHICKEN WITH TARRAGON HONEY BUTTER

This simple yet elegantly flavored dish is something you'll love to serve company!

> 4 boneless skinless chicken breast halves
> 2 tablespoons coarsely crushed multi-colored peppercorns*
> 1/2 to 1 teaspoon kosher (coarse) salt
> 1 tablespoon vegetable oil
> 1/4 cup butter, softened
> 1 teaspoon dried tarragon
> 2 tablespoons honey

❶ Rinse chicken and pat dry. Coat chicken with crushed peppercorns and sprinkle with salt. Place chicken between sheets of plastic wrap and pound lightly with the flat side of a meat mallet until peppercorns are pressed into chicken and chicken is slightly flattened.

❷ In heavy skillet, heat oil over medium-high heat until hot. Add chicken; cook 12 to 15 minutes, turning once, until chicken is no longer pink in center.

❸ In small bowl, combine butter, tarragon and honey; mix until well blended. Spread mixture over chicken breasts.

TIP *To crush peppercorns, crush in a coffee mill, mini food processor or place in small heavy-duty plastic bag. Close bag and pound with meat mallet, rolling pin or empty wine bottle until coarsely crushed.

4 servings.
Preparation time: 5 minutes. Ready to serve: 15 minutes.
Per serving: 310 calories, 18 g total fat (9 g saturated fat), 97 mg cholesterol, 331 mg sodium, .6 g fiber.

ARINATED BROILED CHICKEN THIGHS

Chicken thighs pick up flavor from the spicy marinade. Cook the thighs quickly under the broiler. Accompany them with stir-fried zucchini, bell peppers, onions and tomatoes. Add parsley-and-onion seasoned bread. Serve fresh fruit for dessert.

1/4 cup olive oil
1/4 cup freshly squeezed lemon juice
 1 teaspoon salt
1/2 teaspoon cayenne
 2 garlic cloves, minced
 1 teaspoon minced fresh rosemary or 1/2 teaspoon dried
 4 large chicken thighs
 1 tablespoon chopped fresh parsley

❶ In medium bowl, combine olive oil, lemon juice, salt, cayenne, garlic and rosemary; mix until well blended. Rinse chicken and pat dry. Add chicken to marinade; refrigerate 24 hours.

❷ Heat broiler. Cover roasting pan with aluminum foil; coat aluminum foil with nonstick cooking spray. Arrange chicken in single layer, skin side down.

❸ Broil chicken 5 to 6 inches from heat about 7 minutes. Flip once and broil an additional 8 to 12 minutes until internal thermometer reaches 180°F. Transfer chicken to serving platter. Garnish with parsley.

4 servings.
Preparation time: 10 minutes. Ready to serve: 24 hours, 12 minutes.
Per serving: 350 calories, 23.5 g total fat (5.5 g saturated fat), 107 mg cholesterol, 390 mg sodium, 0 g fiber.

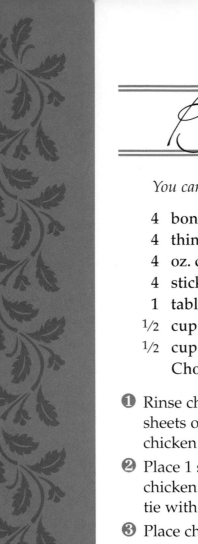

BAKED HAM AND CRAB-STUFFED CHICKEN ROLLS

You can prepare the stuffed chicken breasts up to 24 hours before baking.

- 4 boneless skinless chicken breast halves
- 4 thin slices Danish sandwich ham
- 4 oz. cooked crabmeat
- 4 sticks Monterey Jack cheese
- 1 tablespoon butter, melted
- 1/2 cup reduced-fat sour cream
- 1/2 cup plain yogurt
- Chopped fresh parsley

❶ Rinse chicken and pat dry. Heat oven to 350°F. Place chicken between sheets of plastic wrap and pound with the flat side of a meat mallet until chicken is about 1/4-inch thick.

❷ Place 1 slice ham, 1 oz. crabmeat and 1 stick cheese on each piece of chicken. Roll up tightly, starting from filled side of each piece of chicken; tie with cotton string.

❸ Place chicken roll in lightly greased shallow baking dish. Brush rolls with melted butter. Bake 20 minutes.

❹ Meanwhile, in small mixing bowl, combine sour cream and yogurt; mix until well blended. Spoon mixture over partially baked chicken rolls; bake an additional 20 minutes or until chicken is no longer pink in center. Sprinkle with parsley.

4 servings.
Preparation time: 10 minutes. Ready to serve: 40 minutes.

Per serving: 315 calories, 13 g total fat (6.5 g saturated fat), 130 mg cholesterol, 1060 mg sodium, 0 g fiber.

MUSHROOM-SAUTEED TURKEY TENDERLOIN

This is a super-quick, delicious way to prepare fresh and convenient turkey tenderloins. While the turkey cooks, toss a salad and steam fresh green vegetables such as beans, asparagus or Brussels sprouts.

1½ lb. turkey tenderloins
 2 tablespoons butter
 1 cup sliced mushrooms
 2 garlic cloves, minced
½ cup dry white wine
 1 teaspoon salt
¼ teaspoon freshly ground pepper

❶ Rinse turkey and pat dry. In heavy skillet, heat butter over medium-high heat until melted. Add mushrooms, garlic and turkey. Cook about 5 minutes or until turkey is evenly browned.

❷ Add wine, salt and pepper to skillet; cover and cook an additional 15 minutes or until turkey is no longer pink in center or internal temperature reaches 180°F.

❸ Cut turkey diagonally into ½-inch slices. Spoon mushrooms over each piece.

6 servings.
Preparation time: 10 minutes. Ready to serve: 25 minutes.
Per serving: 185 calories, 7.5 g total fat (3.5 g saturated fat), 77.5 mg cholesterol, 475 mg sodium, 0 g fiber.

BAKED & ROASTED POULTRY

A chicken or turkey in the oven fills a house with an aroma that just makes you feel good. The anticipation builds as the cooking nears completion. And if you've used a good recipe and the right techniques, the end result never disappoints! When you've got a little time, or got things to do while the bird cooks, these are the recipes (twists on the traditional and new ideas too) that will make you feel — and eat — good.

Roast Chicken with Orange and Spices, page 117

CRUNCHY PECAN CHICKEN

This oven-fried chicken is sure to please the family; serve hot or cold.

3¹/2 to 4 lb. chicken pieces, cut up
  ¹/4 cup vegetable oil
  ³/4 cup seasoned bread crumbs
  ¹/2 cup ground pecans
  ¹/2 cup (2 oz.) grated Parmesan cheese.

❶ Heat oven to 400°F. Place a large metal rack over a rimmed cookie sheet; coat with nonstick cooking spray.

❷ Rinse chicken and pat dry. Remove skin if desired.

❸ Pour oil into large bowl. Combine bread crumbs, pecans and cheese on a flat plate.

❹ Lightly brush chicken with oil. Roll chicken in crumb mixture to generously coat. Place coated chicken in single layer on rack over baking sheet.

❺ Bake 40 to 50 minutes or until chicken is no longer pink in center.

6 servings.
Preparation time: 10 minutes. Ready to serve: 50 minutes.

Per serving: 475 calories, 30 g total fat (7 g saturated fat), 100 mg cholesterol, 330 mg sodium, 1 g fiber.

PEPPERED CORNISH GAME HENS

Remove the backbone of each hen to flatten the birds for quick, intense cooking.

4	(1- to 1½-lb.) Cornish game hens
1½	tablespoons sweet Hungarian paprika
½	tablespoon freshly ground pepper
½	tablespoon Szechwan peppercorns, crushed
2	teaspoons olive oil
¼	teaspoon salt

❶ Heat oven to 425°F. Remove giblets from hens; reserve for another use. Rinse hens and pat dry. Remove skins if desired (this greatly reduces the fat).

❷ With poultry shears, cut along both sides of backbone of each hen and remove. Split at breastbone to halve.

❸ In medium bowl, combine paprika, pepper, peppercorns, oil and salt; mix well. Coat meat on both sides with pepper mixture.

❹ Place hens between sheets of plastic wrap and pound with flat side of meat mallet, pressing pepper mixture into surface of hens.

❺ Spray shallow baking pan with nonstick cooking spray; arrange hens in pan, inside down, in single layer. Bake 25 to 30 minutes or until meat is no longer pink in center. Do not turn, but baste with pan juices once or twice during baking.

8 servings.
Preparation time: 20 minutes. Ready to serve: 30 minutes.
Per serving: 315 calories, 22 g total fat (6 g saturated fat), 150 mg cholesterol, 150 mg sodium, .5 g fiber.

MAPLE-GLAZED ROAST TURKEY WITH WILD RICE AND DRIED CRANBERRY DRESSING

With the dressing enclosed in a cheesecloth bag, it is easy to remove from the turkey before serving.

Wild Rice and Dried Cranberry Dressing
1 (14- to 16-lb.) turkey
4 tablespoons butter, melted
1 tablespoon chopped fresh sage
1 tablespoon chopped fresh thyme
1/4 teaspoon salt
1/4 teaspoon freshly ground pepper
2 cups chicken broth
1 tablespoon maple syrup

❶ Prepare Wild Rice and Dried Cranberry Dressing. Cut a piece of doubled cheesecloth 16 inches square; mound dressing on cloth. Tie loosely.

❷ Place rack in lower third of oven. Heat oven to 325°F. Rinse turkey and pat dry.

❸ Place turkey on roasting rack in large roasting pan. Brush with 2 tablespoons butter. Sprinkle with herbs, salt and pepper. Place bag of dressing into cavity of turkey.

❹ Tie legs together with cotton string and tuck wing tip under body. Pour broth into pan and roast turkey 3 hours, basting with pan juices every 30 minutes.

❺ Add maple syrup to remaining 2 tablespoons butter and brush over turkey. Roast an additional 30 minutes or until internal temperature reaches 180°F.

❻ Transfer turkey to serving platter; remove dressing. Cover turkey with aluminum foil; let stand 20 minutes. Pour pan juices into pitcher; skim off fat, discard.

WILD RICE AND DRIED CRANBERRY DRESSING

3	tablespoons butter
1½	cups chopped fresh mushrooms
½	cup chopped onion
¼	teaspoon salt
1	cup dried cranberries
⅓	cup raisins
2	cups cooked wild rice

❶ In large skillet, heat butter over medium heat until melted; add mushrooms and onions. Sauté over medium heat about 10 minutes.

❷ Stir in salt, cranberries, raisins and wild rice; remove from heat.

8 to 10 servings.
Preparation time: 30 minutes. Ready to serve: 4 hours.

Per serving: 475 calories, 24 g total fat (10 g saturated fat), 124 mg cholesterol, 915 mg sodium, 2 g fiber.

ROASTED FIVE-SPICE TURKEY BREAST

Asian five-spice seasoning blend has become a standard in market spice sections today. This is a simple and delicious way to season turkey.

1   (2- to 4-lb.) bone-in turkey breast
1   cup water
4   tablespoons melted butter
1/2   cup honey
1/4   cup Dijon mustard
1/4   cup soy sauce
4   teaspoons Asian five-spice seasoning

❶ Rinse turkey and pat dry. Place breast skin side up on rack in shallow roasting pan. Pour water into pan beneath rack.

❷ Heat oven to 325°F. In large bowl, combine butter, honey, soy sauce, mustard and five-spice; mix until well blended. Rub mixture over turkey, coating all sides.

❸ Roast 2 to 2 1/2 hours or until internal temperature reaches 180°F. Let stand 15 minutes before carving.

6 servings.
Preparation time: 10 minutes. Ready to serve: 3 hours.
Per serving: 390 calories, 18 g total fat (8 g saturated fat), 105 g cholesterol, 940 mg sodium, 1 g fiber.

PERFECTLY SIMPLE ROASTED FREE-RANGE CHICKEN

This recipe is so simple! A sprig of fresh rosemary slipped under the skin perfumes the roast, but it isn't mandatory. Perfect for a dinner party or a family meal, use this basic recipe for roasting any whole chicken, but free-range chicken has so much more natural flavor!

1   (4½- to 7-lb.) whole free-range chicken
3   sprigs fresh rosemary or 1½ teaspoons dried
4   tablespoons butter, cut into 4 pieces
2   teaspoons kosher (coarse) salt
1   teaspoon freshly ground pepper

❶ Rinse chicken and pat dry. Heat oven to 325°F. Loosen skin over breast of chicken and place 1 sprig fresh rosemary or ¼ teaspoon dried plus 1 tablespoon butter on each side of chicken. Place remaining rosemary into cavity of chicken.

❷ Tuck wing tips under chicken and tie legs together with cotton string. Rub remaining butter over chicken and sprinkle with salt and pepper. Place in roasting pan, breast side up. Roast, basting occasionally with pan juices, 20 minutes per pound or until juices run clear and internal temperature reaches 180°F.

❸ Let stand 15 minutes before carving.

5 to 7 servings.
Preparation time: 10 minutes. Ready to serve: 2 hours, 30 minutes.
Per serving: 475 calories, 30 g total fat (11.5 g saturated fat), 174.5 mg cholesterol, 815 mg sodium, 0 g fiber.

CORNISH GAME HENS WITH HERB RUB

Curry powder and chili powder are two key ingredients for this vibrantly flavored treatment for whole game hens. The pan juices are especially good spooned over cooked rice.

2	(1½-lb.) Cornish game hens
1	tablespoon olive oil
1½	teaspoons chili powder
1½	teaspoons curry powder
2	garlic cloves, minced
1	teaspoon kosher (coarse) salt

❶ Heat oven to 350°F. Remove giblets from hens; reserve for another use. Rinse hens and pat dry. In small bowl, combine olive oil, chili powder, curry powder, garlic and salt to make paste; mix until well blended. Rub paste on skin and in cavities of game hens. Tuck wing tips under shoulders and tie legs together with cotton string.

❷ Place hens breast side up on rack in shallow roasting pan. Insert meat thermometer so tip is in thickest part of inside thigh muscle and does not touch bone. Roast, uncovered, 1¼ hours and meat is no longer pink in center or until internal temperature reaches 180°F.

❸ With poultry shears, cut each hen in half.

4 servings.
Preparation time: 20 minutes. Ready to serve: 1 hour, 30 minutes.
Per serving: 335 calories, 25 g total fat (6 g saturated fat), 150 mg cholesterol, 474 mg sodium, 1 g fiber.

OVEN BRAISED TURKEY DRUMSTICKS WITH WHITE BEANS

Turkey drumsticks slow cook to tender succulence with savory beans and vegetables — perfect for a cold weather meal.

1½ cups dried cannellini beans
2 tablespoons olive oil
6 turkey drumsticks (about 3 lbs.)
1 yellow onion, diced
1 rib celery, diced
2 large carrots, diced
6 garlic cloves, minced
1½ cups dry white wine
1½ cups chicken broth
1½ cups peeled, seeded and chopped tomatoes
3 tablespoons tomato paste
1 teaspoon chopped fresh thyme
1 bay leaf
¼ teaspoon salt
¼ teaspoon freshly ground pepper
1 tablespoon grated lemon zest
2 tablespoons chopped fresh parsley

❶ Rinse beans and discard stones; soak overnight in water to cover.

❷ Heat oven to 350°F. In Dutch oven, heat olive oil over medium-high heat. Add turkey; brown on all sides. Stir in onion, celery, carrots, garlic, beans, wine, broth, tomatoes, tomato paste, thyme and bay leaf; sauté 3 minutes. Transfer to casserole; bake for 3 to 4 hours or until meat is very tender and falls off the bone. Add water or more broth if necessary.

❸ Remove from oven; remove and discard bones. Return meat to casserole; season with salt and pepper. Remove and discard bay leaf.

❹ Garnish with lemon zest and parsley.

6 servings.
Preparation time: 15 minutes. Ready to serve: 16 hours.
Per serving: 520 calories, 17 g total fat (4 g saturated fat), 95 g cholesterol, 825 mg sodium, 11 g fiber.

ROAST CHICKEN WITH ORANGE AND SPICES

For an elegant yet simple autumn menu, serve this dish (pictured on page 107) with steamed wild rice, a crisp green salad and freshly baked bread. Bake apples or pears for dessert right along with the chicken!

1	(4- to 4½-lb.) roasting chicken
1	orange
¼	cup butter, softened
1	teaspoon salt
½	teaspoon ground cardamom
½	teaspoon ground cinnamon
¼	teaspoon ground cloves

❶ Heat oven to 450°F. Rinse chicken and pat dry.

❷ Grate 1 tablespoon of peel from orange. In small bowl, combine butter with orange peel, salt, cardamom, cinnamon and cloves; mix well. Rub mixture over chicken, spreading some inside cavity.

❸ Stuff cavity of chicken with whole orange. Tuck wings under chicken, cross legs and tie together with cotton string. Place chicken breast side up on rack in shallow roasting pan.

❹ Roast at 450°F 20 minutes. Reduce temperature to 350°F. Baste with pan juices and roast an additional 40 minutes or until juices run clear and internal temperature reaches 180°F, basting chicken with pan juices 2 to 3 times during roasting.

❺ Transfer chicken to serving platter. Remove orange. Cut orange in half and squeeze juice over chicken; brush chicken with pan juices.

6 servings.
Preparation time: 15 minutes. Ready to serve: 1 hour.

Per serving: 370 calories, 23 g total fat (9 g saturated fat), 132 mg cholesterol, 540 mg sodium, 1 g fiber.

JERK-MARINATED ROASTED DRUMSTICKS

Habañero chiles are hot, that's for sure! But don't ignore this recipe if you don't like Habañeros; just skip them and add a dash of hot pepper sauce instead.

- 8 chicken drumsticks (about 2 lbs.)
- 1½ cups Jamaican Jerk Marinade
  Chopped fresh cilantro

❶ Rinse drumsticks and pat dry. Place drumsticks in resealable plastic bag; add marinade. Refrigerate overnight or up to 24 hours.

❷ Heat oven and roasting pan to 500°F. Remove drumsticks from marinade; place in roasting pan. Roast 25 to 35 minutes or until drumsticks are no longer pink in center.

JAMAICAN JERK MARINADE

- 1 sweet onion, chopped
- 4 green onions, chopped
- 2 tablespoons fresh thyme or 2 teaspoons dried
- 4 teaspoons ground allspice
- 1 teaspoon each salt, ground nutmeg, ground cinnamon and freshly ground pepper
- 1 to 6 Habañero chiles, seeded*
- 4 garlic cloves, peeled
- 2 tablespoons grated fresh ginger
- 2 tablespoons freshly squeezed lime juice
- ½ cup red wine vinegar
- ¼ cup each olive oil, soy sauce and dark rum
- 2 tablespoons packed brown sugar

❶ In food processor, combine sweet onion, green onions, thyme, allspice, salt, nutmeg, cinnamon, pepper, chiles, garlic, ginger, lime juice, vinegar, oil, soy sauce, rum and brown sugar; process until smooth.

TIP *Always wear gloves when seeding Habañero chiles.

4 servings.
Preparation time: 10 minutes. Ready to serve: 24 hours, 30 minutes.

Per serving: 320 calories, 18.5 g total fat (5 g saturated fat), 98 mg cholesterol, 495 mg sodium, 1 g fiber.

OAST CHICKEN WITH GARLIC, HERBS AND BALSAMIC VINEGAR

This simple roast chicken is made all the more succulent by stuffing garlic butter just under the skin.

1 (4- to 4½-lb.) roasting chicken
2 tablespoons butter, softened
3 large garlic cloves, minced
2 teaspoons fresh marjoram leaves
2 teaspoons fresh basil leaves
2 teaspoons fresh rosemary leaves
1 teaspoon salt
½ teaspoon freshly ground pepper
2 tablespoons olive oil
4 tablespoons balsamic vinegar

❶ Heat oven to 375°F.

❷ Rinse chicken and pat dry. Loosen skin from breast of chicken. Loosen skin covering thigh and legs, being careful not to tear the skin.

❸ In small bowl, combine butter, garlic, marjoram, basil, rosemary, salt and pepper; mix until well blended. In another small bowl, whisk together olive oil and 2 tablespoons of the balsamic vinegar; mix well.

❹ With thin rubber spatula, stuff about ¾ of herb mixture between flesh and skin of chicken. Rub outside of skin to smooth out stuffing, kneading it into an even layer. Place remaining herb mixture in cavity of chicken. Rub ½ of vinegar mixture on outside of chicken, place remaining vinegar mixture inside cavity.

❺ Tuck wings under chicken; cross legs and tie together with cotton string. Place chicken with breast side up on rack in shallow baking pan. Pour 1 cup water into pan. Roast, basting occasionally with pan juices 1 to 1½ hours or until internal temperature reaches 180°F.

❻ Remove from oven; cool 10 minutes before carving. Meanwhile, transfer pan juices to medium saucepan. Remove fat; add remaining 2 tablespoons vinegar. Simmer over medium heat 5 minutes. Serve sauce over carved chicken.

6 servings.
Preparation time: 20 minutes. Ready to serve: 1 hour, 40 minutes.
Per serving: 340 calories, 20.5 g total fat (6.5 g saturated fat), 119 mg cholesterol, 310 mg sodium, 0 g fiber.

BAKED BARBECUE CHICKEN LEGS AND THIGHS

This barbecue sauce is simple to put together with ingredients you have in the kitchen cupboard. And it doesn't even require pre-cooking!

3	lb. chicken legs and thighs
1	onion, thinly sliced
1	garlic clove, minced
1	(8-oz.) can tomato sauce
1/4	cup ketchup
2	tablespoons Dijon mustard
1/4	cup honey
1	teaspoon salt
1	tablespoon chili powder
1	tablespoon Worcestershire sauce
1	teaspoon smoke flavoring

❶ Heat oven to 350°F. Spray 13x9-inch baking dish with nonstick cooking spray. Arrange chicken in pan. Top with onion.

❷ In medium bowl, combine garlic, tomato sauce, ketchup, mustard, honey, salt, chili powder, Worcestershire sauce and smoke flavoring; mix until well blended. Pour mixture over chicken. Bake, uncovered, 1 hour or until chicken is no longer pink in center.

6 servings.
Preparation time: 10 minutes. Ready to serve: 1 hour.

Per serving: 355 calories, 16.5 g total fat (4.5 g saturated fat), 101.5 mg cholesterol, 930 mg sodium, 2 g fiber.

CLASSICS

Chicken and dumplings, turkey Tetrazzini, chicken Cacciatore... classic poultry dishes deserve a spot in every cook's menu at some time or another. The recipes here provide a few new wrinkles on these and some other old but still great favorites.

Chicken and Herbed Dumplings, page 130

CHICKEN CACCIATORE

This is an American-Italian dish reminiscent of food prepared "hunter style" with mushrooms, onions, tomatoes, herbs and wine.

1   (3- to 3½-lb.) broiler-fryer chicken, cut up
      All-purpose flour
2   tablespoons butter
2   tablespoons olive oil
2   garlic cloves, minced
1   onion, chopped
1   (14.5-oz.) can whole tomatoes
1   red or green bell pepper, thinly sliced
2   tablespoons chopped fresh parsley
½   teaspoon salt
½   teaspoon dried thyme
½   teaspoon dried oregano
¼   teaspoon freshly ground pepper
1   bay leaf
½   cup dry red wine
½   pound mushrooms, thinly sliced
8   oz. spaghetti

❶ Rinse chicken and pat dry. Coat each piece with flour. Heat butter and oil in large nonstick skillet over medium-high heat until hot. Add chicken, a few at a time, and brown on all sides. Transfer chicken to platter.

❷ Add garlic and onion to pan drippings; sauté 3 to 4 minutes or until just tender, stirring frequently. Return chicken to skillet; add tomatoes, bell pepper, parsley, salt, thyme, oregano, pepper, bay leaf and wine.

❸ Cover and simmer over medium heat about 45 minutes or until chicken is tender and no longer pink in center. Stir in mushrooms. Cover and cook an additional 10 to 15 minutes or until mushrooms are just tender. Meanwhile, cook spaghetti according to package directions; drain.

④ Transfer chicken and vegetables to serving platter. Increase heat to high and boil liquid until reduced and thickened, stirring constantly. Pour sauce over chicken. Garnish with additional parsley; serve chicken and sauce over spaghetti.

4 to 6 servings.
Preparation time: 30 minutes. Ready to serve: 1 hour.

Per serving: 730 calories, 32 g total fat (10 g saturated fat), 140.5 mg cholesterol, 980 mg sodium, 6 g fiber.

TURKEY LOAF WITH SUN-DRIED TOMATOES AND PINE NUTS

This updated version of meatloaf is packed with flavor and low in fat. Serve with mashed potatoes and steamed vegetables. Use this great turkey loaf in sandwiches too!

1¼	lb. ground turkey breast
1	teaspoon salt
½	teaspoon coarsely ground pepper
1	egg
¼	cup chopped green onions
¼	cup sun-dried tomatoes, packed in oil, coarsely chopped
2	tablespoons pine nuts
½	cup fresh packed bread crumbs
½	cup chicken broth

❶ Heat oven to 350°F. Lightly grease 8x3-inch loaf pan.

❷ In large bowl, combine turkey with salt, pepper, egg, onions, sun-dried tomatoes, pine nuts, bread crumbs and broth; mix until well blended. Spread mixture into pan.

❸ Bake 1 hour or until turkey is no longer pink in center. Let stand 10 minutes.

6 servings.
Preparation time: 10 minutes. Ready to serve: 1 hour, 10 minutes.

Per serving: 170 calories, 6 g total fat (1.5 g saturated fat), 91.5 mg cholesterol, 570 mg sodium, 1 g fiber.

COUNTRY CAPTAIN SKILLET

This classic gets its name from an army captain who brought the recipe to England from India. Fused with English ingredients, the recipe traveled with early settlers to the United States where more "fusion" happened when it was combined with available ingredients: chicken, onions and tomatoes. It's now a dish of chicken cooked in a curry-flavored raisin sauce and served over rice, topped with slivered almonds — and it doesn't take all day to prepare!

1	(3- to 3½-lb.) frying chicken, cut up
¼	cup all-purpose flour
1	sweet onion, thinly sliced
¼	cup raisins
2	tablespoons chopped fresh parsley
1½	teaspoons curry powder
½	teaspoon salt
½	teaspoon dried thyme
⅛	teaspoon cayenne
1	red bell pepper, cut into ½-inch pieces
1	green bell pepper, cut into ½-inch pieces
1	garlic clove, minced
1	(14.5-oz.) can diced tomatoes
3	cups hot cooked rice
¼	cup toasted, slivered, almonds
2	tablespoons chopped fresh parsley

❶ Heat oven to 350°F. Rinse chicken and pat dry. Remove skin; coat pieces with flour. Place chicken in heavy casserole with tight-fitting lid.

❷ Add onion, raisins, parsley, curry powder, salt, thyme, cayenne, red bell pepper, green bell pepper, garlic and tomatoes. Cover and bake 1 hour or until chicken is no longer pink in center. Serve hot over rice; sprinkle with almonds and parsley.

6 servings.
Preparation time: 15 minutes. Ready to serve: 1 hour.

Per serving: 350 calories, 8 g total fat (2 g saturated fat), 74 mg cholesterol, 680 mg sodium, 3 g fiber.

TURKEY TETRAZZINI

This dish is named after Luisa Tetrazzini, a famous Italian soprano of the early 1900s. It was created for her by the chef of the Palace Hotel in San Francisco. Although the dish was originally made with chicken, this has become a favorite day-after-Thanksgiving dish using cooked turkey.

4	tablespoons butter
5	tablespoons all-purpose flour
2½	cups reduced-sodium chicken broth
1	cup half-and-half
½	cup dry white wine
¾	cup (3 oz.) freshly shredded Parmesan cheese
8	oz. fettuccine
1	lb. fresh mushrooms, sliced
3 to 4	cups cooked turkey, shredded
½	teaspoon salt

❶ Heat oven to 375°F. Coat 3-quart shallow casserole with nonstick cooking spray.

❷ In 3-quart saucepan, melt 2 tablespoons butter over medium heat; stir in flour. Blend in broth, half-and-half and wine. Cook, about 3 minutes, stirring constantly. Stir in ½ cup of the cheese. Reserve 1 cup of the sauce; add remaining cheese to sauce in pan.

❸ Cook fettuccine according to package directions; drain.

❹ Melt remaining 2 tablespoons butter in heavy skillet over high heat. Add mushrooms; cook, until lightly browned, stirring constantly.

❺ In large bowl, combine sauce, mushrooms, fettuccine, turkey and salt; mix until well blended. Spoon mixture into casserole; spoon reserved 1 cup sauce evenly over top.

❻ Bake 15 minutes or until casserole is hot and bubbly.

4 to 6 servings.
Preparation time: 10 minutes. Ready to serve: 15 minutes.

Per serving: 715 calories, 32.5 g total fat (17 g saturated fat), 198 mg cholesterol, 745 mg sodium, 3.5 g fiber.

CHICKEN AND HERBED DUMPLINGS

Truly comfort food, this old-fashioned dish is just right for a wintry day.

1 (3½- to 4-lb.) whole chicken
2 ribs celery, chopped
2 carrots, peeled, sliced
1 parsnip, peeled, cubed
1 onion, chopped
3 garlic cloves, minced
1 bay leaf
2 teaspoons salt
1 teaspoon dried thyme
1 bunch parsley
½ teaspoon freshly ground pepper

HERBED DUMPLINGS

1 cup all-purpose flour
½ teaspoon dried thyme
½ teaspoon dried marjoram
1½ teaspoons baking powder
½ teaspoon salt
3 tablespoons butter
¼ cup chopped parsley
⅓ cup milk

❶ Remove giblets and neck from chicken; reserve. Rinse chicken and place breast side up in large stockpot. Add celery, carrots, parsnip, onion, garlic, bay leaf, salt, thyme, parsley and pepper; add water just to cover chicken.

❷ Bring water to boil over high heat. Reduce to medium-low, cover and simmer about 50 minutes or until chicken is no longer pink in center. Remove and discard parsley and bay leaf.

❸ In medium bowl, combine flour, thyme, marjoram, baking powder and salt; mix well. Add butter; with fork, blend into flour mixture. Add chopped parsley. With fork, stir in milk to make firm dough. Divide into 10 parts; shape each into dumpling.

❹ Transfer chicken to platter; remove skin; carve into serving pieces and place in deep serving bowl. With slotted spoon, transfer vegetables to chicken. Cover with foil to keep warm.

5 Bring broth in pot to a boil; skim off any foam. With large spoon, lower dumplings into boiling broth. Cover and cook 10 to 15 minutes or until dumplings puff and interiors are uniformly set. To test, cut into center of 1 dumpling.

6 Spoon dumplings over chicken and vegetables; pour the broth over dumplings, chicken and vegetables. Serve in wide soup plates.

6 cups.
Preparation time: 15 minutes. Ready to serve: 1 hour.

Per cup: 340 calories, 12.5 g total fat (5.5 g saturated fat), 93 mg cholesterol, 1230 mg sodium, 3 g fiber.

CHICKEN, MUSHROOM AND SPINACH PIE

Not only does this dish look pretty, but the combined flavors of mushrooms, spinach and a bit of basil are very pleasing. Use the frozen chicken breasts that come in a bag, or select fresh ones from the meat counter. Just be aware that frozen breasts might be a bit saltier.

PASTRY

- 1½ cups all-purpose flour
- ½ cup butter, chilled, sliced
- 1 egg, beaten
- 3 tablespoons ice water

FILLING

- ¼ cup butter
- 3 garlic cloves, minced
- 1 lb. fresh mushrooms, sliced
- 1 lb. boneless skinless chicken breasts, rinsed, cut into 1-inch pieces
- ½ cup water
- 3 tablespoons cornstarch
- 1 teaspoon dried basil
- 1 teaspoon instant chicken bouillon granules
- ¼ teaspoon freshly ground pepper
- ½ cup sliced almonds
- 1 (10-oz.) pkg. frozen chopped spinach, thawed, squeezed to drain well

❶ In food processor, combine flour and butter; pulse 8 to 10 times, until butter is sliced into pea-size pieces. In small bowl, beat egg and ice water with fork until well blended; reserve 1 teaspoon of mixture.

❷ Add remaining mixture to flour-butter mixture; process until dough forms a small ball. Divide into 2 parts; wrap and refrigerate 30 to 60 minutes. Heat oven to 400°F.

❸ In 10- to 12-inch heavy skillet, melt ¼ cup butter over high heat; add garlic, mushrooms and chicken. Stir frequently 6 to 8 minutes or until chicken is no longer pink in center. Meanwhile, in small bowl, combine water, cornstarch, basil, bouillon and pepper; mix until well blended. Add to mushroom-chicken mixture. Cook, stirring constantly, about 1 minute until thickened. Remove from heat.

④ On a floured work surface, roll 1 part of pastry to make 12-inch round; fit into 9-inch pie plate. Sprinkle sliced almonds over bottom. Roll out second ball of dough to make 12-inch round; set aside.

⑤ Place chicken-mushroom mixture over almonds in pan. Add spinach in an even layer over chicken.

⑥ Place second round of pastry over top. Moisten edges and turn under; crimp to seal. Brush top with reserved teaspoon egg mixture. Make 8 to 10 small cuts on top of pie.

⑦ Bake 30 to 35 minutes or until pastry is golden. Let stand 15 to 20 minutes.

8 servings.
Preparation time: 30 minutes. Ready to serve: 2 hours.

Per serving: 385 calories, 23 g total fat (12 g saturated fat), 104 mg cholesterol, 335 mg sodium, 3 g fiber.

GRILLING & BARBECUING

The rubs, bastes, glazes and marinades here — used in conjunction with the handy poultry grilling chart on page 145 — will let you make a wide variety of truly juicy, flavor-filled poultry meals on the grill. You'll love the other recipes here too.

Chicken and Shrimp Kabobs with Poblano Chile Sauce, page 148

GRILLING & BARBECUING POULTRY

Take your pick of poultry — chicken, turkey or game hens — cut up into pieces, halved, quartered or whole. All are candidates for grilling and barbecuing. Because poultry is so versatile, relatively quick to cook and simple to handle, there is a world of flavor choices for the palate that craves variety.

For a spur-of-the-moment meal, select chicken or turkey breast pieces and a flavorful rub or baste, and follow the guidelines for cooking poultry in the *Basic Poultry Grilling Times and Techniques* table (page 145). Grilled poultry that is simply seasoned with salt and pepper also can be finished off with a special glaze.

For meals that you plan ahead, you may wish to season your meat choice in a zesty marinade up to 24 hours before grilling. The grilling times and techniques remain the same.

The following rubs, bastes, glazes and marinades can be used interchangeably.

SPICY RUBS AND BASTES:

All of the bastes are sufficient for a 3 1/2- to 4-lb. chicken (whole, cut up, or boneless and skinless); two Cornish game hens; one whole turkey breast; or 2 to 3 pounds of turkey tenderloins.

CHILI PEPPER RUB   *Pictured at right*

- 1 teaspoon chili powder
- 1 teaspoon paprika
- 1/4 teaspoon cayenne
- 2 tablespoons vegetable oil
- 2 teaspoons Dijon mustard

❶ In small bowl, combine chili powder, paprika, cayenne, oil and mustard; mix until well blended. Brush mixture over poultry occasionally while grilling. Follow grill chart on page 145 for grilling instructions.

4 servings.
Preparation time: 5 minutes.

Per serving: 35 calories, 4 g total fat (.5 g saturated fat), 0 mg cholesterol, 39.5 mg sodium, .5 g fiber.

HERB AND SAKE RUB

    1 cup chopped fresh celery leaves
    1 cup chopped fresh cilantro
    1 teaspoon chopped fresh rosemary
  1/2 cup sake or sherry
    2 tablespoons vegetable oil

❶ In food processor, combine all ingredients; process until coarsely chopped. Rub mixture over poultry; grill immediately, or refrigerate up to 4 hours. Follow grill chart on page 145 for grilling instructions.

4 servings. Preparation time: 5 minutes.

Per serving: 115 calories, 7 g total fat (1 g saturated fat), 0 mg cholesterol, 12 mg sodium, 1 g fiber.

CURRY-SEASONED BUTTER BASTE

  1/4 cup butter, melted
    4 teaspoons curry powder
  1/4 teaspoon ground ginger
  1/4 teaspoon ground cloves
  1/4 teaspoon fresly ground pepper
    1 teaspoon crushed red pepper flakes

❶ In small bowl, combine all ingredients; mix until well blended. Brush mixture over poultry occasionally while grilling. Follow grill chart on page 145 for grilling instructions.

4 servings. Preparation time: 5 minutes.

Per serving: 210 calories, 25 g total fat (14 g saturated fat), 60 mg cholesterol, 155 mg sodium, 1 g fiber.

CHINESE HOISIN-HONEY BASTE

  1/4 cup hoisin sauce
  1/4 cup honey
  1/2 teaspoon sesame oil
  1/2 teaspoon kosher (coarse) salt
  1/2 teaspoon freshly ground pepper

❶ In medium saucepan, combine all ingredients; mix well. Cook over medium-high heat 3 minutes or until mixture is liquid. Brush mixture over poultry occasionally while grilling. Follow grill chart on page 145 for grilling instructions.

4 servings. Preparation time: 5 minutes.

Per serving: 101 calories, 1.3 g total fat (.2 g saturated fat), 0 mg cholesterol, 200 mg sodium, .7 g fiber.

SPICY ASIAN BASTE

 2 tablespoons fresh orange juice
 1 tablespoon lemon juice
 1 teaspoon hoisin sauce
1/2 teaspoon Chinese chili paste
 1 teaspoon grated fresh ginger
 2 garlic cloves, minced

1 In small bowl, combine all ingredients; mix until well blended. Brush mixture over poultry occasionally while grilling. Follow grill chart on page 145.

4 servings. Preparation time: 5 minutes.

Per serving: 10 calories, 0 g total fat (0 g saturated fat), 0 mg cholesterol, 2 mg sodium, 1 g fiber.

DIJON HONEY MUSTARD BASTE

1/4 cup Dijon mustard
1/4 cup honey
 1 teaspoon salt
1/2 teaspoon coarsely ground pepper

1 In medium saucepan, combine all ingredients. Cook over medium-high heat 3 minutes or until mixture is liquid. Brush mixture over poultry occasionally while grilling. Follow grill chart on page 145 for grilling instructions.

4 servings. Preparation time: 5 minutes.

Per serving: 75 calories, 1 g total fat (0 g saturated fat), 0 mg cholesterol, 780 mg sodium, .5 g fiber.

LEMON AND GARLIC BASTE

1/4 cup lemon juice
1/4 cup puréed garlic
1/4 cup butter, melted
1/2 teaspoon each salt and pepper

1 In small bowl, combine all ingredients; mix until well blended. Brush mixture over poultry occasionally while grilling. Follow grill chart on page 145 for grilling instructions.

4 servings. Preparation time: 5 minutes.

Per serving: 120 calories, 11.5 g total fat (7 g saturated fat), 30 mg cholesterol, 370 mg sodium, 7 g fiber.

GLAZES FOR FINISHING:

Glazes provide a shiny exterior and tasty finishing flavor to poultry. It is important to save glazing until the last 5 minutes of grilling to avoid burning.

FRESH PEACH GLAZE   *Pictured at right*

3	large ripe peaches, peeled, pitted, diced or 3 cups sliced frozen peaches, thawed
1/4	cup packed brown sugar
1/4	cup fresh orange juice
1	tablespoon grated orange peel
2	tablespoons minced crystallized ginger
1	green onion, chopped
3	tablespoons dry white wine
3/4	teaspoon curry powder

❶ In medium saucepan, combine peaches, brown sugar, orange juice, orange peel, ginger, onion, white wine and curry powder; mix until well blended. Heat over medium heat; simmer 20 minutes, stirring often. Pour into food processor; process until smooth. Brush mixture over hot, grilled poultry occasionally during last 5 minutes grilling time. Follow grill chart on page 145 for grilling instructions.

4 servings.
Preparation time: 10 minutes.

Per serving: 130 calories, 0 g total fat (0 g saturated fat), 0 mg cholesterol, 22.5 mg sodium, 3 g fiber.

COFFEE-COCOA GLAZE

1/4	cup butter
1/3	cup very strong coffee
1/4	cup bottled steak sauce
1	tablespoon unsweetened cocoa powder

❶ In medium saucepan, combine butter, coffee, steak sauce and cocoa powder. Bring to a simmer over medium-high heat; simmer 1 minute or until sauce is thick and smooth. Brush mixture over hot grilled poultry frequently during last 5 to 10 minutes grill time. Follow grill chart on page 145 for grilling instructions.

4 servings.
Preparation time: 5 minutes.

Per serving: 115 calories, 12 g total fat (7 g saturated fat), 31 mg cholesterol, 305 mg sodium, 1 g fiber.

MARINADES:

SPICY MOROCCAN MARINADE *Pictured at right*

- ¼ cup olive oil
- 1 teaspoon sesame oil
- 1 teaspoon ground coriander seeds
- ½ teaspoon ground cinnamon
- 2 teaspoons ground cumin
- ½ teaspoon ground turmeric
- ½ teaspoon paprika
  Dash cayenne
- 1 tablespoon grated fresh ginger
- ½ teaspoon kosher (coarse) salt
- 1 tablespoon lemon juice

❶ In medium saucepan, combine olive oil and sesame oil; heat over medium-high heat until hot. Stir in coriander, cinnamon, cumin, turmeric, paprika and cayenne. Cook about 1 minute or until spices are aromatic; add ginger, salt and lemon juice. Rub mixture over poultry, coating all sides. Place in covered container and refrigerate overnight. Follow grill chart on page 145 for grilling instructions.

4 servings.
Preparation time: 10 minutes.

Per serving: 35 calories, 4 g total fat (1 g saturated fat), 0 mg cholesterol, 50 mg sodium, 0 g fiber.

INDONESIAN MARINADE

- 1 garlic clove
- 1 small onion, quartered
- 2 tablespoons each water and vegetable oil
- ½ teaspoon crushed red pepper flakes
- 6 tablespoons soy sauce
- 2 tablespoons sugar
- 2 tablespoons lemon juice
- ¼ teaspoon freshly ground pepper

❶ Combine garlic, onion, water and oil in food processor; process until smooth. Pour mixture into medium saucepan. Cook at medium heat 10 minutes, stirring constantly; remove from heat. Whisk in red pepper flakes, soy sauce, sugar, lemon juice and pepper. Pour over poultry and coat all sides. Place in covered container; refrigerate overnight. Follow grill chart on page 145 for grilling instructions.

4 servings.
Preparation time: 10 minutes.

Per serving: 27 calories, 2 g total fat (1 g saturated fat), 0 mg cholesterol, 385 mg sodium, 1 g fiber.

GINGER SOY MARINADE

1/3 cup soy sauce
1 cup white wine
1 garlic clove, minced
1 tablespoon sugar
2 tablespoons lemon juice
3 tablespoons grated fresh ginger
1/4 cup sesame seeds

❶ In small bowl, combine soy sauce, wine, garlic, sugar, lemon juice, ginger and sesame seeds; mix. Pour mixture over poultry. Cover and refrigerate overnight. Grill using guidelines on grilling chart.

4 servings. Preparation time: 10 minutes.

Per serving: 32 calories, 1 g total fat (0 g saturated fat), 0 mg cholesterol, 340 mg sodium, 1 g fiber.

GARLIC AND ORANGE MARINADE

3 large garlic cloves, minced or pressed
1/2 cup olive oil
1 to 1 1/2 teaspoons grated orange zest
1/2 teaspoon dried rosemary

❶ In small bowl, combine garlic, oil, orange zest and rosemary; mix. Pour mixture over poultry. Cover and refrigerate overnight. Grill using guidelines on grilling chart.

4 servings. Preparation time: 10 minutes.

Per serving: 60 calories, 7 g total fat (1 g saturated fat), 0 mg cholesterol, 0 mg sodium, 0 g fiber.

HERB-MUSTARD MARINADE

1/2 cup dry white wine
2/3 cup vegetable oil
6 tablespoons white wine vinegar
2 tablespoons finely chopped onion
1 teaspoon mixed Italian herbs
2 garlic cloves, minced
1/2 teaspoon freshly ground pepper
1/4 cup spicy brown mustard

❶ In small bowl, combine wine, oil, vinegar, onion, herbs, garlic, pepper and mustard; mix. Pour mixture over poultry. Cover and refrigerate overnight. Grill using guidelines on grilling chart.

4 servings. Preparation time: 10 minutes.

Per serving: 90 calories, 10 g total fat (1 g saturated fat), 0 mg cholesterol, 50 mg sodium, 0 g fiber.

BASIC POULTRY GRILLING TIMES AND TECHNIQUES

Type of Poultry	Weight	Grilling Method	Fire Method	Doneness Temperature	Cook Time
CHICKEN					
Whole	3-5 lbs.	Indirect	Hot/banked	180°F	1 - 1¼ hrs.
	6-7 lbs.	Indirect	Hot/banked	180°F	1½ - 1¾ hrs.
Halved/quartered	3-4 lbs.	Direct	Medium	No pink meat near bone	40-50 min.
Butterflied	3-5 lbs.	Direct	Medium	No pink meat near bone	45-55 min.
Cut up	3-4 lbs.	Direct	Medium	No pink meat near bone	35-40 min.
Breast halves, bone-in	8-12 oz. each	Direct	Medium	No pink meat near bone	15-25 min.
Whole legs, leg & thigh	8-10 oz. each	Direct	Medium	No pink meat near bone	35-45 min.
Drumsticks	4-6 oz. each	Direct	Medium	No pink meat near bone	30-35 min.
Thighs	4-6 oz. each	Direct	Medium	No pink meat near bone	30-35 min.
Wings	3-4 oz. each	Direct	Medium	No pink meat near bone	25-30 min.
ROCK CORNISH GAME HEN					
Whole	1 - 1½ lbs.	Indirect	Hot/banked	No pink meat near bone	45-60 min.
Halves	1½ lbs. total	Direct	Medium	No pink meat near bone	30-40 min.
TURKEY					
Whole	9-15 lbs.	Indirect	Hot/banked	180°F	15 min./lb.
Halved	10-12 lbs.	Indirect	Hot/banked	180°F	1½ - 2 hrs.
Breast halves with bone	10-12 lbs.	Indirect	Hot/banked	180°F	1 - 1½ hrs.
Drumsticks/thighs	1-2 lbs. each	Direct covered	Medium	No pink meat near bone	55-65 min.
Boneless cubes	1 inch	Direct	Medium	No pink meat when cut	12-15 min.
Breast steaks	½-inch thick	Direct	Medium	No pink meat when cut	7-9 min.

GRILLED CHICKEN BREAST WITH ROSEMARY AND SUN-DRIED TOMATO PESTO

This may become a classic in your chicken-grilling repertoire. The flavors of the marinade permeate the chicken, and render it succulent and juicy as well.

4 boneless skinless chicken breast halves
1 tablespoon fresh lemon juice
2 teaspoons finely chopped fresh rosemary
1 teaspoon minced garlic
1 teaspoon kosher (coarse) salt
1/2 teaspoon freshly ground pepper
  Rosemary sprigs, if desired
  Sun-Dried Tomato Pesto

❶ Rinse chicken and pat dry. In large, heavy resealable plastic bag, combine lemon juice, rosemary, garlic, salt and pepper. Place chicken in bag, coating all sides with lemon juice. Seal bag; refrigerate 30 minutes.

❷ Place chicken on gas grill over medium-high heat or on charcoal grill 4 to 6 inches from medium-high coals. Cook 10 minutes or until chicken is no longer pink in center, turning once. Garnish with rosemary and Sun-Dried Tomato Pesto.

SUN-DRIED TOMATO PESTO

1/2 cup sun-dried tomatoes packed in oil
1/4 cup pine nuts
  1 cup packed fresh basil leaves
1/2 cup (2 oz.) grated Parmesan
1/4 cup olive oil
1/4 cup chopped garlic

❶ In food processor, combine sun-dried tomatoes, pine nuts, basil leaves, Parmesan, oil and garlic; process until roughly chopped.

4 servings.
Preparation time: 10 minutes. Ready to serve: 40 minutes.

Per serving: 410 calories, 27 g total fat (6 g saturated fat), 76 mg cholesterol, 730 mg sodium, 2 g fiber.

CHICKEN AND SHRIMP KABOBS WITH POBLANO CHILE SAUCE

Consider this dish when you plan a menu for company and you'd like to prepare things in advance. Assemble the skewers and marinate them in the refrigerator at least 1 hour or up to 24 hours.

- 2 boneless skinless chicken breast halves
- 12 shelled, deveined, uncooked, jumbo shrimp
- 2 small zucchini, cut into 1/2-inch slices
- 4 wooden skewers
- 2 tablespoons butter, melted
- 1 tablespoon honey
- 1 tablespoon lemon juice
- 2 teaspoons chili powder
- 1/4 teaspoon cayenne
  Poblano Chile Sauce

1 Rinse chicken and pat dry. Thread 4 (8- to 10-inch) skewers with 2 pieces of chicken and 3 shrimp, separated by pieces of zucchini. Place skewers in 13x9-inch glass baking dish.

2 In small bowl, combine butter, honey, lemon juice, chili powder and cayenne; mix until well blended. Pour mixture over skewers. Cover and refrigerate 1 hour, turning skewers occasionally.

3 Meanwhile, prepare Poblano Chile Sauce.

4 Heat grill. Remove skewers from marinade; discard marinade. Lightly oil grill rack. Place skewers on gas grill over medium heat or on charcoal grill 4 to 6 inches from medium coals. Serve with Poblano Chile Sauce.

POBLANO CHILE SAUCE

- 1/2 lb. fresh poblano chiles*
- 2 red bell peppers
- 3 teaspoons vegetable oil
- 2 garlic cloves, chopped
- 1 large onion, chopped
- 1 cup chicken broth
- 1/2 teaspoon salt

❶ Heat oven to 500°F. Line baking sheet with foil.

❷ Rub chiles and bell peppers with 1 teaspoon oil. Place on baking sheet; roast 6 to 10 minutes or until skins are blistered and have brown patches, turning 2 to 3 times.

❸ Transfer chiles to small bowl; cover and let stand until cool enough to handle. Peel chiles and bell peppers, cut off tops and discard seeds and ribs. (Use protective gloves when handling chiles.)

❹ Place garlic in 1-cup measuring cup; add onion to fill measuring cup. In heavy skillet, heat remaining 2 teaspoons oil over medium heat. Add garlic and onion, cook about 3 minutes, stirring frequently until softened. Stir in broth and chiles; simmer 1 minute. Place broth mixture in food processor; process until completely smooth. Cut bell peppers into 1/2-inch pieces; add to sauce. Season with salt.

TIP *You can find Poblano chiles in Latino markets and many supermarkets.

4 servings.
Preparation time: 30 minutes.
Ready to serve: 1 hour.

Per serving: 310 calories, 10 g total fat (3.5 g saturated fat), 190 mg cholesterol, 1070 mg sodium, 3 g fiber.

CHICKEN MARINATED IN YOGURT WITH LEMON AND PEPPER

Long, slow marinating in garlicky yogurt tenderizes, moistens and adds flavor, so you can enjoy grilled chicken that's delicious as well as low in fat. Serve with soft pita bread or flatbread, and steamed rice.

 2 large garlic cloves, minced
 1/2 teaspoon salt
 2 cups plain whole-milk yogurt
 1/4 cup lemon juice
   Pulp of 1 large lemon
 1/2 teaspoon freshly ground pepper
 2 large bone-in chicken breasts

❶ In large shallow bowl, stir together garlic, salt, yogurt, lemon juice, lemon pulp and pepper. Remove skin and fat from chicken. Rinse chicken and pat dry. Bend breasts backward to break bones so pieces lie flat. Add chicken to yogurt mixture; turn to coat all sides.

❷ Cover bowl tightly; refrigerate at least overnight, turning once or twice.

❸ Remove chicken from marinade; discard. Place on gas grill over medium-high heat or on charcoal grill 4 to 6 inches from medium coals. Cook 12 to 16 minutes on each side or until no longer pink in center, turning once. Meat should be well browned but not burned.

6 servings.
Preparation time: 30 minutes. Ready to serve: 12 hours.

Per serving: 140 calories, 3.5 g total fat (1.5 g saturated fat), 62 mg cholesterol, 110 mg sodium, 0 g fiber.

LEMON-LIME GRILLED CHICKEN WITH HERBS AND SPICES

The tartness of citrus and the aroma of herbs lend great flavor to boneless chicken breasts. Cook them in a ridged grill pan on the stovetop when you can't barbecue outdoors.

1/4	teaspoon coriander seeds
1/4	teaspoon fennel seeds
1/3	cup honey
3	tablespoons lemon juice
2	tablespoons lime juice
1	green onion, minced
1/2	teaspoon dried thyme
1/2	teaspoon dried rosemary
1/2	teaspoon dried fresh sage
4	boneless skinless chicken breasts (about 1½ lb.)
1/2	teaspoon salt
1/2	teaspoon freshly ground pepper

❶ In heavy skillet, toast coriander seeds and fennel seeds over medium heat about 4 minutes or until fragrant. In large bowl, pulverize toasted seeds with mortar and pestle; mix with honey.

❷ Whisk in lemon juice and lime juice, onion, thyme, rosemary and sage. Add chicken, turning to coat both sides; cover and refrigerate 8 hours.

❸ Heat grill. Remove chicken from marinade; sprinkle with salt and pepper. Place chicken on gas grill over medium-high heat or on charcoal grill 4 to 6 inches from medium-high coals. Cook 7 minutes, turning once, or until chicken is no longer pink in center.

4 servings.
Preparation time: 10 minutes. Ready to serve: 8 hours, 7 minutes.
Per serving: 165 calories, 3.5 g total fat (1 g saturated fat), 66 mg cholesterol, 350 mg sodium, 0 g fiber.

CHILI-COCONUT MARINATED GRILLED TURKEY TENDERLOIN

Turkey tenderloins cook quickly, and are quick to absorb wonderful flavors. Serve them sliced, accompanied with a tropical fruit salsa made of chopped mango, fresh pineapple, fresh papaya, red onion and cilantro.

MEAT

　　4　turkey breast tenderloins

CHILI-COCONUT MARINADE

　　1/2　small onion, chopped
　　3　tablespoons minced fresh cilantro
　　2　tablespoons minced fresh ginger
　　3　large garlic cloves, peeled
　　1　teaspoon lemon peel
　1/4 to 1/2　teaspoon crushed red pepper flakes
　　1/2　cup lite soy sauce
　　1/2　cup unsweetened coconut milk
　　3　tablespoons vegetable oil
　　1　tablespoon sugar
　　　Chopped fresh cilantro

❶ Rinse turkey and pat dry. Place in 13x9-inch baking dish.

❷ In food processor, combine onion, cilantro, ginger, garlic, lemon, red pepper flakes, soy sauce, coconut, oil and sugar; process until smooth. Pour mixture over turkey; coat evenly. Cover with plastic wrap; refrigerate at least 8 hours. Bring to room temperature before grilling.

❸ Heat grill; lightly oil grill rack. Remove turkey from marinade; discard marinade. Place turkey on gas grill over medium-high heat or on charcoal grill 4 to 6 inches from medium-high coals. Cook 14 to 16 minutes or until turkey is no longer pink in center, but still juicy. Place on cutting board; cover with aluminum foil. Let stand 5 minutes. Cut 1/2-inch-thick diagonal slices. Garnish with cilantro.

6 servings.

Preparation time: 10 minutes. Ready to serve: 8 hours, 20 minutes.

Per serving: 225 calories, 7.5 g total fat (2.5 g saturated fat), 90 mg cholesterol, 285 mg sodium, 0 g fiber.

ALDER- AND ROSEMARY-SMOKED WHOLE TURKEY

Chunks of green or water-soaked alder provide a marvelously aromatic smoke in which to cook rosemary-stuffed turkey. If you do not have alder, add soaked mesquite chips to the fire during the smoking. This would be a great method to prepare a wild turkey.

1 (16- to 18-lb.) turkey
4 fresh rosemary sprigs plus rosemary sprigs for garnish
3 tablespoons olive oil
2 tablespoons minced fresh rosemary
1 tablespoon minced Italian or regular parsley
12 oz. alder pieces, green or soaked in water

❶ Remove and discard leg truss from turkey. Remove neck and giblets; reserve for another use. Remove and discard fat. Rinse turkey and pat dry. Place 4 sprigs of fresh rosemary inside cavity. Close with small metal skewers; tie legs together with cotton string. Turn wing tips under.

❷ In small bowl, combine olive oil, rosemary and parsley; mix until well blended.

❸ Heat grill. For charcoal grill, place foil pan under cooking grate and on top of heat source. Place alder pieces in foil pan.

❹ Place turkey breast side up in center of cooking grate. Cover grill; cook 2 to 3 hours or until internal temperature reaches 180°F, adding additional alder pieces after 30 minutes. If parts of the turkey get too dark, cover those areas loosely with foil.

❺ Transfer turkey to serving platter; cover loosely with foil. Let stand 15 minutes. Garnish with rosemary sprigs.

16 to 18 servings.
Preparation time: 10 minutes. Ready to serve: 3 hours.

Per serving: 190 calories, 4.5 g total fat (1.5 g saturated fat), 87.5 mg cholesterol, 265 mg sodium, 0 g fiber.

LEMON-SAGE MARINATED CORNISH GAME HENS

Hens are perfect with this lemon-sage marinade. You can also grill quartered broiler-fryer chicken pieces using this same marinade. You'll need two 3-pound chickens, quartered, for eight servings.

4 (1½-lb.) Cornish game hens
¾ cup fresh lemon juice
6 tablespoons olive oil
¼ cup vodka, if desired
¼ cup fresh sage leaves or 1 tablespoon dried, crumbled
2 teaspoons honey
   Dash hot pepper sauce

❶ Rinse game hens and pat dry. Split, removing backbone. Place in large resealable plastic bag. In small bowl, combine lemon juice, olive oil, vodka, sage, honey and hot pepper sauce; mix together until well blended. Pour mixture into bag, coating hens completely. Seal bag; marinate in refrigerator 24 hours.

❷ Heat grill. Remove hens from marinade; discard marinade.

❸ Place hens skin side down on gas grill over medium-high heat or on charcoal grill 4 to 6 inches from medium-high coals. Cook 30 minutes, turning once, or until internal temperature reaches 180°F.

8 servings.
Preparation time: 10 minutes.
Ready to serve: 24 hours, 30 minutes.

Per serving: 360 calories, 26 g total fat (6.5 g saturated fat), 150 mg cholesterol, 80 mg sodium, 0 g fiber.

POULTRY & PASTA

Although not traditionally thought of as complements, poultry combines beautifully and naturally with a wide variety of pasta. The secret, of course, lies in the sauce you make to bring everything together, and in how you cook the components. Here are the recipe ideas you'll need to create great meals out of chicken or turkey, and pasta.

Turkey with Spinach Tortellini and Fresh Oranges, page 163

BAKED CHICKEN AND TOMATOES WITH FETTUCCINI

Here's an easy dish almost all families will enjoy. The chicken is baked on a bed of tomatoes. While it bakes, make a simple tomato sauce for the top.

1 (14¹/₂-oz.) can diced tomatoes in tomato purée
1 (3¹/₂-lb.) chicken, cut up
2 large garlic cloves, slivered
¹/₃ cup coarsely chopped fresh flat-leaf parsley
¹/₄ teaspoon salt
³/₄ teaspoon pepper
¹/₂ cup olive oil
12 oz. fettuccini
¹/₄ cup freshly grated Parmesan cheese
Simple Tomato Sauce

❶ Heat oven to 400°F. Spread diced tomatoes in 9x13-inch baking dish.

❷ Rinse chicken and pat dry. Arrange chicken on top of tomatoes with skin-side down. Tuck garlic slivers between chicken; sprinkle with parsley, salt and pepper. Drizzle ¹/₄ cup olive oil over top.

❸ Bake chicken about 30 minutes or until brown on one side; turn and brown other side until chicken is no longer pink in center. If tomatoes start to dry out, add water to pan.

❹ Cook fettuccini according to package directions. Drain.

❺ Remove chicken from oven and spread fettuccini over chicken. Sprinkle with Parmesan cheese; cover with sauce and bake an additional 10 to 15 minutes or until sauce is bubbly.

SIMPLE TOMATO SAUCE

2 large garlic cloves, smashed
2¹/₂ cups canned chopped tomatoes
¹/₂ teaspoon salt
1¹/₂ tablespoons chopped fresh basil or 1¹/₂ teaspoons dried

❶ In medium saucepan, warm remaining ¹/₄ cup olive oil and garlic over medium-low heat until garlic is golden. Add tomatoes, salt and basil. Simmer 15 minutes. Pour mixture into food processor; process until smooth. Reheat just before serving. Season with salt and pepper.

6 servings.
Preparation time: 20 minutes. Ready to serve: 45 minutes.

Per serving: 700 calories, 38.5 g total fat (8.5 g saturated fat), 150.5 mg cholesterol, 2000 mg sodium, 3.5 g fiber.

CHICKEN LASAGNA WITH NO-BOIL PASTA AND THREE CHEESES

A fabulous lasagna for cheese lovers.

2	tablespoons olive oil
1	lb. ground chicken or turkey
1	large onion, finely chopped
1	red bell pepper, seeded, finely chopped
3	garlic cloves, minced
1/8 to 1	teaspoon cayenne
2	(15-oz.) cans diced tomatoes with herbs
1/4	teaspoon each salt and pepper
1	(15-oz.) carton ricotta cheese
3	cups shredded mozzarella cheese
1/2	cup freshly grated Parmesan cheese
1	egg
1	tablespoon dried parsley flakes
1/2	lb. lasagna noodles

❶ Heat oven to 350°F. Coat 2-quart shallow 8x10-inch or 7x11-inch lasagna pan with nonstick cooking spray.

❷ In heavy skillet, heat oil over medium-high heat until hot; add chicken. Cook, about 5 minutes, stirring occasionally until browned. Add onion and bell pepper; cook an additional 2 minutes. Add garlic and cayenne; cook an additional 30 seconds. Stir in tomatoes and bring to a boil. Reduce heat; simmer about 20 minutes or until sauce has thickened. Season with salt and pepper.

❸ In a large bowl, combine ricotta, 2 cups mozzarella cheese, Parmesan cheese, egg and parsley; mix well.

❹ Spread 1 cup of tomato mixture in lasagna pan. Top with 3 uncooked lasagna noodles placed side-by-side. Spread 1/3 of ricotta mixture over noodles and sprinkle with 1/3 cup of mozzarella cheese. Spoon 1/4 of remaining sauce over cheese. Repeat layering, placing lasagna noodles in opposite direction with each layer. Top with remaining mozzarella cheese.

❺ Cover and bake about 30 to 35 minutes or until heated through and sauce is bubbling. Remove lasagna from oven; cool 10 minutes before serving.

6 servings.
Preparation time: 15 minutes. Ready to serve: 1 hour, 15 minutes.

Per serving: 700 calories, 35.5 g total fat (17 g saturated fat), 160 mg cholesterol, 1190 mg sodium, 3.5 g fiber.

PASTA WITH TURKEY MEATBALLS

Turkey meatballs served with cooked pasta and fresh tomato create a light variation on traditional meatballs, and make a wonderful meal to savor.

MEATBALLS

1 to 1½	lb. ground turkey breast
1	small yellow onion, finely minced
2	garlic cloves, minced
2	teaspoons finely chopped fresh oregano or ½ teaspoon dried
2	teaspoons finely chopped fresh basil or ½ teaspoon dried
2	teaspoons finely chopped fresh rosemary or ½ teaspoon dried
1	large egg
⅓	cup fine dry bread crumbs
⅓	cup chopped fresh flat-leaf parsley
1	teaspoon salt
½	teaspoon freshly ground pepper

SAUCE

1	(28-oz.) jar spaghetti sauce with herbs
1	tomato, diced
12	oz. penne or ziti
½	cup freshly grated Parmesan cheese

❶ Heat oven to 500°F. Cover 15x10x1-inch pan with aluminum foil and coat with nonstick cooking spray.

❷ In large bowl, combine turkey with half of onion; add garlic, oregano, basil, rosemary, egg, bread crumbs, parsley, salt and pepper; mix until well blended. Shape into 24 (1-inch) meatballs. Arrange mixture in single layer on foil-covered pan. Bake 10 minutes or until meatballs are no longer pink in center.

❸ Meanwhile, in large saucepan, combine spaghetti sauce with tomato; heat to boiling. Add meatballs and pan drippings to sauce.

❹ Cook pasta according to package directions. Drain and add to meatball mixture. Sprinkle cheese over top.

4 to 6 servings.
Preparation time: 15 minutes. Ready to serve: 30 minutes.

Per serving: 815 calories, 20.5 g total fat (6 g saturated fat), 165 mg cholesterol, 2690 mg sodium, 7.5 g fiber.

CHICKEN AND VEGETABLES WITH PASTA

This is such a versatile recipe, you'll find many ways to vary it. Select different pasta varieties, and vegetables that are in season.

- 8 oz. multi-colored rotelle or penne rigate pasta
- 2 tablespoons olive oil
- 1 lb. boneless skinless chicken breast halves, rinsed and cut into 1-inch pieces
- 1 garlic clove, minced
- 5 cups seasonal vegetables*
- 4 green onions, chopped
- 1/4 can sun-dried tomatoes, packed in oil, drained
- 6 plum tomatoes, diced (1/2-inch thick)
- 1 teaspoon dried basil
- 1/2 teaspoon pepper
- 2 teaspoons freshly grated lemon peel
- 1 tablespoon fresh lemon juice
  Freshly grated Parmesan cheese
  Toasted pine nuts

❶ Cook pasta according to package directions. Drain.

❷ Meanwhile, in heavy skillet, heat 1 tablespoon oil over medium-high heat until hot. Add chicken; cook, about 4 minutes or until chicken is no longer pink in center. Set aside.

❸ Add remaining 1 tablespoon oil, garlic, vegetables and onions to skillet; toss over high heat 4 to 6 minutes or until vegetables are tender. Reduce heat to low. Stir in chicken, tomatoes, basil and pepper; cook about 1 minute or until chicken is warm. Remove from heat; add lemon peel and juice.

❹ Toss pasta with chicken and vegetables. Serve with Parmesan cheese and toasted pine nuts.

TIP *Seasonal vegetables may include: zucchini, broccoli florets, fresh asparagus, and carrots julienne.

4 servings.
Preparation time: 10 minutes. Ready to serve: 25 minutes.
Per serving: 555 calories, 19 g total fat (4 g saturated fat), 65 mg cholesterol, 450 mg sodium, 7.5 g fiber.

TURKEY WITH SPINACH TORTELLINI AND FRESH ORANGES

This is a great way to serve leftover cooked turkey. Buy fresh cheese-filled spinach tortellini in the market's dairy section.

  3 large seedless oranges
  7 cups homemade turkey or chicken broth
1½ pounds fresh cheese-filled spinach tortellini
  3 cups cooked, diced or shredded turkey
  2 cups sour cream
  2 green onions, thinly sliced
     Freshly shredded Parmesan cheese

❶ With vegetable peeler, remove 6-inch x 1-inch strip of peel from all 3 oranges. Cut strips into long, thin shreds and set aside. Peel oranges; cut crosswise into ¼-inch slices. Arrange slices on edges of serving platter.

❷ In 8-quart stockpot, bring broth to a rolling boil. Add tortellini; cook according to package directions. Remove tortellini; set aside and keep warm.

❸ Add turkey and orange peel shreds to broth; cook just until turkey is heated through. Remove turkey; add to tortellini.

❹ In small skillet, combine sour cream with ½ cup broth and green onions; mix well. Heat mixture until just warm.

❺ Spoon tortellini and turkey onto orange-lined serving platter; spoon sauce over tortellini. Serve with Parmesan cheese.

6 servings.

Preparation time: 10 minutes. Ready to serve: 20 minutes.

Per serving: 485 calories, 25.5 g total fat (14 g saturated fat), 202 mg cholesterol, 135 mg sodium, 3 g fiber.

ROTELLE WITH GRILLED CHICKEN AND GARLIC-CHEESE SAUCE

Rotelle are spiral-shaped pasta. Farfalle or "bow-tie" pasta can be substituted. Don't expect a thick coating of sauce, but just enough to flavor and moisten the pasta, broccoli and chicken.

4	boneless skinless chicken breast halves
1	tablespoon olive oil
10	oz. dry rotelle
2	cups broccoli florets
1/4	cup dry white wine
1	garlic clove, minced
1	green onion, thinly sliced
1	cup whipping cream
1/4	teaspoon salt
1/2	cup freshly shredded Asiago or Parmesan cheese
	Chopped fresh basil
	Asiago or Parmesan ribbons*

❶ Rinse chicken and pat dry. Brush chicken evenly with oil.

❷ In heavy skillet, heat oil over medium-high heat until hot. Place chicken in pan and cook, about 5 minutes, turning once on each side or until chicken is no longer pink in center. Cut chicken crosswise into 1/2-inch strips.

❸ Meanwhile, in 6-quart stockpot, cook pasta according to package directions. Add broccoli during last 3 minutes of cooking time. Drain pasta and broccoli; set aside.

❹ In large skillet, heat wine, garlic and onion over medium heat about 2 minutes, stirring constantly, until bubbly. Stir in cream. Season with salt. Stir in broccoli-pasta mixture, chicken and shredded cheese.

❺ Garnish with chopped fresh basil and cheese ribbons.

TIP *To make cheese ribbons, peel a block of cheese using potato peeler. Garnish each serving with 1 or 2 curls.

4 to 6 servings.
Preparation time: 15 minutes. Ready to serve: 30 minutes.

Per serving: 700 calories, 30 g total fat (16 g saturated fat), 144 mg cholesterol, 640 mg sodium, 4 g fiber.

CHICKEN AND SPINACH RAVIOLI WITH GARLIC PESTO SAUCE

To vary the flavor and make the meal even easier, create this recipe with any of the refrigerated pesto sauces available.

- 4 boneless skinless chicken breasts, rinsed, cut into 2-inch cubes
- 2 tablespoons olive oil
- 2 cups fresh pea pods
- 1 small zucchini, cut diagonally into 1/4-inch slices
- 1 red bell pepper, seeded, cut into 1/4-inch strips
- 1 (9-oz.) pkg. spinach ravioli
- 1 (7-oz.) pkg. prepared garlic pesto sauce
- 1/4 cup freshly shredded Parmesan cheese

❶ In heavy skillet, heat olive oil over medium-high heat until hot. Add chicken and stir-fry 5 to 6 minutes or until chicken is no longer pink in center.

❷ To skillet add pea pods, zucchini and bell pepper; stir-fry an additional 5 minutes or until vegetables are crisp-tender.

❸ Meanwhile, cook ravioli according to package directions. Drain and add to chicken and vegetables. Add pesto sauce; toss until well mixed. Sprinkle with the Parmesan cheese.

4 servings.
Preparation time: 10 minutes. Ready to serve: 30 minutes.

Per serving: 625 calories, 40.5 g total fat (9 g saturated fat), 155.5 mg cholesterol, 875 mg sodium, 4.5 g fiber.

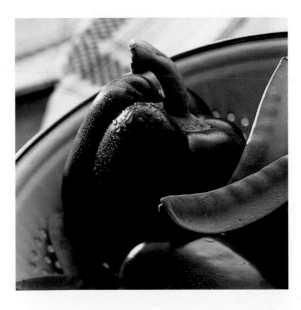

RECIPE INDEX

This index lists every recipe in Pure Poultry *by name. If you're looking for a specific recipe but can't recall the exact name, turn to the General Index that starts on page 168.*

GENERAL INDEX

There are several ways to use this helpful index. First — you can find recipes by name. If you don't know a recipe's specific name but recall a main ingredient or the cooking technique, look under that heading and all the related recipes will be listed; scan for the recipe you want. If you have an ingredient or cooking technique in mind and want to find a great recipe for it, look under that heading as well to find a list of recipes to choose from. Finally — you can use this general index to find a summary of the recipes in each chapter of the book (appetizers, soups, salads, etc.).